TAKEN

Sue O'Callaghan

GETAWAY PUBLISHING NZ

First edition published 2015
by Getaway Publishing NZ
PO Box 32 165
Devonport, Auckland 0744
NEW ZEALAND

Email: info@taken2003uk.com
Web: www.taken2003uk.com
Facebook: taken2003uk

ISBN   978-0-473-34072-8 (paperback)
        978-0-473-34074-2 (hardback)
        978-0-473-34073-5 (epub)
        978-0-473-34075-9 (kindle)
        978-0-473-34076-6 (pdf)

Cover photo by Dreamstime
Typeset in Adobe Garamond Pro
Book design: Bozidar Jokanovic

DEDICATION

This book is dedicated to my four remarkable children Harry, Annie, Alfred and Alice.

You are the greatest gift that life could have bestowed on me. Your courage to push through, your perseverance to endure, your tenacity to overcome, your deep knowledge and understanding of life, and most of all your ability to forgive, have all borne witness to the tremendous love that is within you. Your hearts are so huge. Your individual gifts, desires, idiosyncrasies and passions will take you far to reach out to those around you as you trust, respect, honour and accept people for who they are—no matter what their circumstances.

As you mature into your destiny and calling never forget what a blessing you are. Remind yourselves always that your tears have watered the good seeds you have sown. These tears were also the catalyst which will allow a harvest of rich abundance to be reaped in your own lives and in the lives of the future generations.

May the desires of your hearts be granted.

'Stop your crying and wipe away your tears.
All that you have done for your children will not go unrewarded.
They will return from the enemy's land.
There is hope for your future.
Your children will come back home'.
—JEREMIAH 31: 16,17 GNT

Contents

ACKNOWLEDGEMENTS

In publishing this book I would firstly like to acknowledge the love and support I received from very dear friends and family who surrounded me during 2003 and 2004, when not only my world collapsed around me, but also the world of my four small children. Without you, we would not be living the life of freedom and joy that we are so grateful for today. Each one of you helped lift us up during some very dark times and gave us the hope and courage to push through. Against all allegations you believed in me as a mother, a person and a friend. You enabled us to not only fight for justice, but also empowered us to pick up the pieces and start again, when we were broken through and through. The lifeline you offered us was a ray of light that sustained us all and one that we will be eternally grateful for.

Secondly, I would like to thank those who have encouraged me to write this book, to tell the story and to reach out to others who have struggled with a similar violation of their rights as a parent, in having to watch their children suffer. Your encouragement has enabled me to get this far.

In particular I wish to acknowledge all those who have helped fund *Taken*, especially the following who have given so generously:

Brently Ford, Anna Cullen, Lucy Anstey, Ingo Lambrecht, Anne O'Callaghan, Helen Brown, The Laking Family, The Sharplin Family, Mike and Anna Webster, Sally Wyatt.

Note

All the names of individuals mentioned in this book have been changed to protect the individuals concerned and release them from being identified. The author is identified in the text as 'Lily', for example. Criticisms of individuals and institutions are the author's honest opinion based on the facts as presented in this book or in court files, or known to her at the time of writing.

CHAPTER ONE

On the 1st of October 2003 my husband returned from work unusually early, collected the children, went for a walk and never returned. It was the most devastating day of my life. What was about to unravel in the next few days and weeks was the beginning of a catastrophic series of events that would earmark radical change in all of our lives. It was one that would transition us into a dimension where we would never be the same again.

I hadn't realised that anything significant had taken place until Social Services arrived unannounced, mid-afternoon, on my doorstep, with their distinguishing large black carry bags which alerted me to suspicion. Furthermore I was innocently ignorant that my husband, Jonathan O'Shea and his family had been collaborating with a psychiatrist in private practice, as well as Social Services for the previous nine months, skillfully, yet so destructively, behind my back. I was totally oblivious to the knowledge, that on the advice of the psychiatrist, Social Services had told him to leave with the children and never return. Not only that but as part of the plan that had been going on between him and his parents, they insisted my husband leave to an 'undisclosed address' where he was to change all numbers and take no calls on his mobile. I was not to discover the children's whereabouts for fifteen days. I didn't even know if they were dead or alive.

I hadn't stopped to ask why Social Services were in my house, who had called them, or at what point they had a right to visit, remaining naively unaware of what was surreptitiously unfolding. They asked where the rest of the family were, deceiving me into believing they did not know.

I was feeling a deep sense of confusion, which I perceived was rooted in evasive and misleading information being communicated to me by the women presently in my house. The exchange we had at this time, unbeknown to me, became the first of many ambiguous conversations, followed by a whole catalogue of fabricated untruths, which over the next thirteen months would unravel like a ball of string that was unsettlingly long. I had unknowingly transitioned from being a full time mum, into starring in the lead role for a drama that Social Services and my husband's family had put together many months earlier, involving my children and I, and following a script I had no knowledge of.

There was no dramatic argument or face to face row that one would expect at the particular moment a husband walks out and leaves his wife and I remained innocently unaware that our marriage of six years had come to an abrupt end, that my husband had left and my children had gone. Jonathan had told me he was going for a walk, as he strapped Alfred—still only a baby—into the buggy. He informed me he would collect our second child Annie from a friend's house where she was playing at the time, and then pick up

Harry our eldest, who was in his first year at the little infant school at the end of the road.

It was six o'clock by the time I became nervous enough to call the police because not only had Social Services not returned, as they had said they would, but neither did the children, nor their father. By my watch, school had ended over three hours ago and even if they had caught up with friends in the village, or stopped by at someone's house on the way back, they would still have been home by the children's dinner time. Jonathan's mobile went straight onto the answer phone, suggesting it was either switched off or that something more sinister had happened.

The police arrived promptly, attending the property and were meticulous in requesting information on each child before taking a full statement. They departed saying they would call me upon receiving any information back at the station. I was distressed and nervous, my assumption being that they had been in an accident as I had no other information to work with, least of all that my husband had taken the children and left. I imagined they would have police cars out searching or that some news would arrive from a hospital saying they had been found. Time was a painful reality, a ticking eternity of biting worries about the welfare of Jonathan and our precious children. It became a waiting game I was sure would bring me terrifying news. I ached. I shook. I paced the house. I could not eat, nor sit, nor stand. I picked up the phone but couldn't think of who to speak to. I put the phone down and paced again.

Eventually it was a call from the police station that triggered my heart to race so rapidly it felt like it was running on a powerful battery supply, pumping and beating to a speed I was not accustomed to. At the same time I felt adrenaline rush around, having a dramatic effect on my body. The officer spoke, "I am afraid we have child protection on our files and so we are not allowed to disclose any information to you. We can be of no further assistance."

My heart stopped. "What is child protection?" I asked. "What does that mean?"

Alarmingly he replied, "I am afraid we are not able to discuss anything with you but suggest you speak with Social Services." My mind flitted to how Jonathan had been acting strangely for a while, and yet I was still in denial, hoping he wasn't having an affair because he was behaving so very differently from the man I had married. He had distanced himself from me, was coming home in the early hours of the morning most days, laughing at me a lot and was being evasive in his conversation. He had been in constant communication with his parents and having meetings behind my back, of which he would not speak. I remembered how only three months earlier he had taken the children without warning and left the house. Fear hit me, as though a cricket ball had struck me on the head and I understood immediately why his attitude and conduct had changed.

My fingers fumbled on the phone's keypad, tripping over themselves to dial the number. It was nine in the evening and Social Services were not there, their recorded message communicated it was 'out of hours' and gave me the times they were open. Out of hours? How could anything be out of hours when my children were gone and I had no idea if they were dead or alive, or whether they were injured or safe? The only service that I was told could possibly help was closed until the following day.

That night didn't exist. I wished it hadn't got dark, as it cruelly reminded me that I was meant to sleep but couldn't. I felt physically sick and there was no emergency number I could call to find the whereabouts of my three children aged one, three and five. Alfred, who had only recently celebrated his first birthday, was still breastfeeding and lived on my hip almost twenty four hours a day, adoring the intimacy of the close bond with his mother. I stood where he should have been asleep in his cot, but it was now surreally empty, the space filled with his tiny pyjamas and little dressing gown, still neatly folded. All of his teddies appeared restless and disturbed, as though they were intuitively aware in their fairy-tale world that something was disturbingly wrong.

In the room next door, Annie's pink cosy bed was eerily empty too. Her toys and dolls lay overly-organised and tidy for a little girl who played with them all each night. Harry's bed beside was barely visible, covered in his cuddly animals who appeared to be looking for him, as they like me, knew he should be snugly tucked under the covers, securely asleep for the night. I went from room to room but there were no sleeping children. My mind raced, wondering if I would ever see them again, flitting from thought to speculation, from accident to injury or—worse still—dead and yet undiscovered, as otherwise I would have heard some news. I couldn't seem to rationalise the truth of the situation as ridiculous as it seemed, because although I had heard 'child protection' from the police, I still panicked.

There was an eerie silence in the air, and the emptiness smelt of death. As the rest of the world slept, I wondered who I could call. Emergency numbers were for fire, casualty, accident or danger but where were the emergency numbers for missing children if the police couldn't help?

My body viciously rejected sleep and my eyes could not bear to catch a glimpse of the clock that my ears acknowledged ticked so loudly. I longed for it to say eight thirty in the morning so I could leave and go and knock on the door of Social Services and be the first to meet with them when they arrived. Had my clock stopped working as well? Each minute took an hour to arrive and each hour passed like days, as my heart missed beats and the sun refused to rise.

I would have loved to have been assured that this was to be the longest night of my life, but little did I know that there were many more to come. How on earth I was to get through them, I was yet to discover.

When the time eventually came, there was no getting up or getting dressed to do. I had been up pacing through the night and was still fully clothed and frantic for the moment that had come. I walked expeditiously out of the door and down to the offices in Twickenham, realising only then that the car had gone as though to hinder my every step. Annoyingly my walking pace was so much slower than the speed at which wheels could have transported me to where I was so keen to be.

By now I wanted to empty my head of all the tedious questions that had poured into my mind during the last eighteen hours, which were irritatingly whizzing around as though on a carousel wheel spinning at top speed. The words 'Social Services' which had cadaverously haunted my head all night, seemed to glow like neon lights above the doorway of the ugly, redbrick eighties building. I wondered whether the people that worked for this English institution would manifest the same hostility that I nervously sensed before even stepping inside.

I passed the local children walking to school which I resented, as their presence seemed to insinuate that it was a normal day, but it wasn't because I was not taking Harry to school, he was not here and conceivably never would be. What if I didn't ever walk him to school again? Or hold his hand as I did each day, pushing Alfred in the buggy as little Annie held on beside?

The glass entrance opened automatically, formidably sliding to let me through, as if sensing my arrival and I was met by a lady sitting behind reception typing as though there was no urgency to the day. I made eye contact with her expectantly assuming she would know exactly who I was and tell me where my children were, explain what child protection meant and make me a cup of tea, telling me everything would be alright.

I told her my name and waited. I waited and I waited. No one saw me. She told me that everyone was either busy and or that no one was in. I asked the lady again, telling her my children had gone and that the police had told me to speak with someone here, but no one wanted to know. I felt a sense of injustice and insisted that someone here needed to see me and that I couldn't leave until they had, but I faced the same reserved, detached gaze before walking out of the door in utter amazement at the absurdity of the situation.

I returned home and picked up the phone, calling them again and again, insisting I would continue to do so until someone other than a lady on reception would agree to speak with me. After four attempts, I was told to come and meet with a Sasha Mumford the following morning. I was shocked; confused by how they operated at Social Services. I wondered whether they did they not know anything about me or my children, or if indeed my conversation with the police the previous night had not actually taken place and my mind had invented the whole present state of affairs.

I left the house; it was obscenely quiet. I walked into Richmond and couldn't believe the town centre had not been closed with barrier signs or road blocks at every main street, as surely someone was searching for my children. I was surprised to see everyone carrying on with their day as if nothing had happened when my whole world had stopped. Mothers held their children's hands which I could not do. They carried their babies which I had spent the past five years enjoying. They shopped as if they had someone to cook for when I didn't. Worse still there were children everywhere, little ones the ages of mine who were wearing the same uniform that little Harry would have worn.

Why I was in Richmond I did not know, as it was a painful place to be, but where else would I go? I could walk to the park and watch mothers push children on swings, or stroll by the river and watch as they happily fed the ducks as mine would be doing at this time of day. Richmond at least had clocks on walls but even these showed no evidence of time passing. I walked home and had the second empty, cold, prolonged and painful night. Longing was the only thing I experienced and was the exclusive word that could describe the desperation of all I felt.

Day three arrived as slowly as day two had left. Finally I shook hands with the Sasha Mumford I had been told to meet when I had pressurised Social Services enough on the phone, convinced I was only passed on so that the poor receptionist never need hear my distraught voice again. I sat down as promptly directed by this woman in front of me, noticing her body language created the impression that she was rather austere and uninterested in my predicament. I sensed the mood in the room to be hostile and morose, and the bland style of male dress displayed before me identified this officer as the mould of female I assumed did this job. At last I was faced by a staff member who was paid to tell me what was going on and answer the many questions I had written as an exhaustive list. The paper was worn and tatty as I had added to it many times, having nothing else to focus on for the past forty five hours.

I was tiring now following two nights of no sleep, and feeling weak as my body had rejected even the sight of food. I hoped there would be a listening ear and someone who would take the time to explain all that had happened, communicate the answers I could not yet anticipate and bring the news of the whereabouts of my children.

I hadn't even looked at the face of the person I shook hands with, as I was mixed with such conflicting emotions; from reserved relief since entering the building, to piercing terror as to what I would hear. Eventually my eyes adjusted from discerning from her clothes what my intuition was saying and glanced long enough to look up and encounter another devastating blow. I focused and saw the face of someone who—if it were not for her hair colour—resembled the distant and rather formal appearance of my mother-in-law. She had also had a career in children's Social Services and her job I knew was not dissimilar to the woman in front of me now. Sasha's age, build, haircut, glasses, demeanour and facial expressions all duplicated that of my husband's mother, who I had always hoped did not depict a stereotype of the average employee in the profession.

As if shock could throw any more jolts, this one hit me like the impact of an earthquake and focused my attention only on the fragility of the ground I was standing on. I looked away and looked back; convinced she was my husband's mother who on many occasions had openly discussed the removal of children from their families. I remembered my heart breaking each time she recounted the stories as we sat in her home, of children being taken from a mother, or siblings separated as they were placed in care. As I listened I would often wonder what role she would play in potentially being a catalyst for tragedy, in what I sensed was a system or an organisation that was failing these families so very badly. This Sasha Mumford reminded me distinctly of these past thoughts in my mind, my only other initiation into the world of child care services and I felt a nauseating feeling of 'deja-vu', wondering what I was silently being told. My intellect was still telling me that this officer's character would be one of empathy and compassion, or of honour and gentleness, but I felt she spoke down to me, belittled me, lectured me and my stomach churned in disbelief that the situation could get any worse.

As though unable to hear, on top of all my other exhaustive lists of flaws, I sensed that this lady was not interested my questions: "Where are my children?" "What is child protection?" "Are they alive?" "What is going on?" I sat solemnly in a rather putrid, decomposing, wool lined chair and felt the confusion vibrating from all the other vulnerable mothers and fathers who presumably had trembled too in this very spot. I saw them in my imagination as pawns, releasing the deepest of emotions a parent could feel, at the mercy of those who seemingly had no right to enter so aggressively into all of our lives.

I sensed too, the disbelief at the news and lack of information that these parents had heard. I thought the windows would crack under the strain and pressure I felt in that room as the following words were announced:

> *"If you make any attempt to contact your children we will put them into care. We want you to have an immediate mental health assessment at the Hamlet Hospital in Richmond. We warn you not to do anything silly."*

CHAPTER TWO

Prior to the children being taken I had been exposed to a sneak preview of the intimidation I was to later face, ironically preparing me for the experience that was yet to be revealed. It was as though I had been lowered gently into lukewarm water before the heat was turned too high.

About three months earlier, before Alfred was even one, and barely a crawling baby, I returned home from a doctor's appointment to find a note on the kitchen table. To my surprise there was no one at the house, and only the existence of my husband's handwriting on a small piece of paper which lay atop our beautiful dining table, gave an indication as to where Harry, Annie and Alfred were:

> *"Gone to my parents and have taken the children. Feel it is not okay for you have them right now."*

Following repeated bouts of sickness which included weight loss, anaemia and general fatigue, I had sought medical advice from my general practitioner. She was a well-respected doctor who had seen me through my last two pregnancies and practiced locally only a few streets away from our house, near where Harry until recently, had attended a little Montessori Nursery School. I had visited the surgery several times previously and was following up on blood tests to try and find the root of these various debilitating symptoms. Whatever the cause, she now mentioned with conviction the possibility of an autoimmune disorder relating to my stomach (later diagnosed as coeliac disease) and booked me in to see a gastroenterologist at the next available appointment.

The note perilously sitting in my hand was not an offer to care for the children for me—not that I desired that because I adored being with them—nor did there seem to be a loving motive behind my husband's removal of the children. The handwritten scrawl, held nervously between my fingers, reinforced the feeling that I did not sense the compassion of someone who loved me, nor the care of a partner by my side. I felt sadness and loneliness, as lately Jonathan had been disengaging himself from me, choosing to spend more and more time with his parents and our Filipino amah, with whom he ate in the evenings instead of me, laughed with, talked to and admired. I saw she also had gone.

I placed the note back where I had found it and immediately jumped in the car and drove the two hour journey to Dorset, assuming the others had travelled by train. It was early evening and the journey was the last thing that I needed at that time, but I was especially concerned that the children had been taken without saying goodbye. I was worried what would this mean to them all, particularly Alfred who was still breastfeeding at night. I knocked on the door of my in-laws and caught a glimpse of Harry's delighted face as he saw me through the front window of the Victorian house that had belonged once to the village school next door, and sat in and amongst surrounding fields, with far stretching views beyond.

Jonathan's parents, Michael and Dorothy were distant people, never really accepting me into the family. They disliked my English middle class background as it went against their extreme political views. Despite their impression of me however, I was surprised that they disgracefully responded to my knock by stating that they would call the police if I did not leave immediately. At this point Harry shouted my name, obviously offended by what he had just heard and as he saw me ran to open the door to let me in. I picked him up to cuddle him and felt the relief in his little body as it clung to mine. I found Alfred who was crying and took him tightly into my arms, both of them showing visible signs of distress at being removed from me without any warning.

The police arrived not long after, having indeed received a call from the household and I was ushered by a young officer upstairs into the bathroom where Annie was lying in the bubbly water playing with ducks. Another officer remained downstairs to chat to my husband and his parents, who had clearly ostracised themselves from me in a different part of their home.

It was a strange feeling facing police questioning in a house where I had stayed many times with my in-laws, with whom I had tried on numerous occasions to build a lasting and strong relationship. I had welcomed opportunities to have them to stay in our apartment in Singapore where we first lived, remembering my affection for my own maternal grandparents, the only ones who were still alive when I was born. I hadn't even questioned the fact that my children would know any lesser love from the generation above, who I had always admired for their patience, wisdom and gracious hospitality. We had invited Michael and Dorothy a few times to stay over the Christmas period, with Michael's mother too, whom I adored. I did the things that I wrongly assumed would help build a bond between a young wife who had no mother and a mother-in-law who had no daughter. I took her shopping, I treated her to cafés and had her to stay for periods of time in our house in London so she could meet our friends and become part of the life we were building.

I hoped she and I would build the relationship I could not have with my own mother, who had passed away many years before. However it was not to be. On all these occasions I remained acutely aware that somehow I wasn't uniting through my conversations, nor my efforts to connect. I felt some deep feelings of dislike coming my way whenever I tried to converse or open up, making myself vulnerable in her presence for the sake of building trust. I was curious why she objected so strongly to my presence and felt a sad loss at the relationship that could have benefitted us both. I wondered if it was because she lived in an all-male world with four sons, no sisters and few female friends, guessing somewhere I rocked the unknown feminine world, which she seemingly played little role in.

The hostility that felt rooted somewhere a long way back in my husband's family compared poorly to the unity I felt with my own relatively large collection of cousins, aunts and uncles. My dear mother had been extremely maternal, loving the three girls she had brought into the world less than three years apart.

She had been a twin and I grew up gratefully mindful of the love between this generation that was transferred so radiantly from women who seemed to do nothing other than disseminate joy from the life they lived. They delighted in being family and we knew of few friends outside the circles they kept, simply because of the numbers of relations there were. They shared together the pleasures of gardens of herbaceous borders and rose arbours brimming with all varieties of scents and pastel shades. There were vegetable gardens always overflowing with the pickings for a meal and fruit trees laden with enough apples and pears to keep us going all year. As children we knew of family get-togethers playing with cousins, where we climbed trees and listened to aunts and uncles tell stories from the eclectic lives they had lived.

I was wrong to have assumed I was to become part of my husband's family and integrate in a similar way to what I had known in mine. Sadly such diversity in our backgrounds, combined with the dynamics between the personalities of the individuals involved, meant I was not a daughter, but was to remain the girl their son had married. My conception of family as I had understood it was soon to be ripped apart and this unwelcome visit was to be the last time I would ever set eyes on the paternal grandparents of my children, not for want of trying. I, the mother of their grandchildren, was regarded as an intruder in their home who they wanted removed by the police.

After questioning me as to why I was there and what was going on, the officer reported that I should be allowed to stay with my children or return to our house in Twickenham with them that night. I instantly not only longed for the security of our own home but could suddenly smell the comfort of the refuge the children knew as their only place of residence. The police, not surprisingly, seemed quite taken aback that the grandparents of my children wanted me removed in such an inhospitable and objectionable manner. I could sense empathy in the officer's eyes, who had spent a while listening to all that had taken place. His smile was gentle as I sat on the floor answering his questions, whilst also reassuring Annie as she suspiciously played in the bath. Alfred was sitting on my lap and Harry was splashing the water as much as he could, to draw attention to the fact he as well, was picking up on the negative atmosphere in the house. Facing so much hostility in their home, I suddenly felt undeserving of the warmth shown by the young man in uniform, whose gentle sensitivity caused tears to swell in the corners of my eyes. In reality, it was absurd that a little girl of only three having fun in the water, alongside her two brothers in the room, should witness their mother face such animosity and I felt my stomach churn as the distress of the situation hit.

I had become accustomed to an increasingly contentious environment in the past few months. There had been a rise in the number of conversations taking place between my husband and his parents, which openly criticised me as a mother, wife and person. At times in the past nine months I felt like my husband was married to his mother, rather than me and I wondered why she featured so influentially in his life. I was beginning to doubt myself and my self-confidence was at an all-time low.

This was the family I had longed for and who I had assumed were an extension of the children I had brought into the world. I thought they would be the very people who would be there to protect us as a newly married couple, look after us, encourage us and love us as a family. Instead they were the very ones who were now taking advantage of our vulnerability and the division that had entered our relationship. They were ostensibly driving a wedge further between their son and I, at a time when their support could have easily turned a stressful situation into one that would be reassuring for not only us as parents, but more importantly for the children who were at such a young age. A tangible sense of the awful truth sank in. I was alone in this and my sole aim currently was to protect our children and be the best mother I could to them in these harsh and rejecting circumstances.

With police present, Jonathan agreed that we should all return to London, but once the two officers in uniform were out of the door he announced we would go in the morning. My heart sank. He was angry. My in-laws were stomping around the house and the Filipino girl, Maya, who had returned from Singapore with us so we could offer her a decent home, pampered to everyone's needs, while I silently cried inside wondering at the loneliness that I felt right then.

I had given birth to three babies in the previous four years and was contending with the worry of an undiagnosed illness, whilst at the same time breastfeeding and facing sleepless nights—the kind of issues that dominate the lives of many young mums. I treasured my children and spent my days devoted to them, raising them as my mother had me, with love, tenderness and complete adoration. Yet I felt isolated and afraid, and conceivably hurt that my husband was not by my side. As my mind became active in thought, I played with Annie, bathing her, drying her and cuddling her, whilst I sat on the bathroom floor breastfeeding Alfred, who was frightened as he had picked up on the tension of all that was going on. I prolonged the exercise for as long as I could while the rest of the household cooked and ate their meal. Several hours passed and I told stories to the older two children as I cuddled them in bed and kissed them goodnight.

All of a sudden, there was nowhere for me to go, the bedrooms were not mine and Alfred needed a calming night time feed. Two hours had passed and in the hope that all had settled and the situation was calmer I thought it in my best interest to show my face. I thought my mind was blowing the events out of all proportion and really it was not as bad as I had imagined. I ventured downstairs, hoping my actions would present as a peace offering and sat on the sofa amongst the four adults who were there. I said nothing but fed Alfred and stroked his head, hoping the knife that was cutting the atmosphere would do something to break the silence.

The knife came down indeed, as Michael, Jonathan's father, turned to me and said, "Look at you! I see evil pouring out of you. Evil is pouring out of your head." The tears suddenly rolled down my face as I could no longer contain them, and I felt disappointment at myself that they had without warning revealed themselves like an overflowing dam that had held back water for an exceedingly long time.

I remained silent and continued to feed Alfred but the pain cut through like an axe and my stomach—already tenderly sore—churned. Could my husband, who was lying on the floor, not respond? Could he not take my hand and lead me away? Could he not protect the woman he married or the mother who was feeding his child? He said nothing. The discomfort was raw and deep and shock prevented the very panic attack that it too was causing.

I left the room and lay on the bed upstairs with all three little ones and silently sobbed. My beautiful babies slept and I felt utterly lost. I longed not to be there. I yearned to be anywhere else with my children, but was trapped until their father agreed we could leave. It was a long night as I lay awake waiting for the dawn to appear—a foreshadowing perhaps of the many nights I would confront in the future as I waited for my abducted children's return. It was as though I needed to be prepared for the long haul ahead and tonight had evolved into a preliminary exposure to what I would later face. I watched the minutes of the clock and ached for the sleep that never came.

The morning brought strained laughter in the kitchen as the children were fed, Maya and Jonathan were offered coffee, and breakfast was passed around to everyone except me. I waited as I hungered, while time once again stood still and the clock ticked louder than it had the night before. I had missed out on dinner and Alfred cried in frustration as my milk did not produce, but I sat with him in his ill-temper and comforted him the best I could.

Jonathan was annoyingly irritated and banged everything lying around as though needing to draw attention to the fact I did not please him. My very presence infuriated him and it could have been no clearer than if it had been written across the wall. He threw things around as he repacked the bags he had previously filled and every movement was diverted my way as if to exasperate the intensity of the resentment he felt. He then threw the keys at me and said, "You drive. I had no sleep last night."

Obediently I sat at the wheel as he manhandled the children into the car and spoke softly as to where Maya should sit. His presence next to me frightened me and yet I hoped the adrenalin generated from the fear would allow me to drive safely through the hunger and fatigue that nauseously niggled. He was not a small man by any means but instantly he seemed to dominate every space both physically and emotionally.

I drove cautiously, but Jonathan's frustration at being a passenger and not in control lasted not more than fifteen minutes when, startling the children once again, he shouted for me to pull over so that he could drive. As I expected Maya climbed into the seat next to him and I took the back seat, which meant I could comfort the children strapped beside. I was not prepared for what followed.

With an outburst of craziness he put his foot down furiously and zig-zagged the car dangerously back and forth across the road, as if he was a mad man in a frenzy behind the wheel. The children screamed and the fear within me grew like a triffid that plagued every part of my being. I felt his temper was not short of a rage which revealed he had the ability to injure us all in the car that day.

When eventually the nerve-racking two hour journey ceased and we finally arrived back in our house in London, home for the first time surprisingly did not feel safe. There was no space which was not monopolized by Jonathan's presence or his prevailing instructions, and my attempt to pretend all was well for the children's sake was interrupted by his forthright instructions to obey him and do what I was told. He shook his finger at me telling me I was mentally ill and 'had it all coming to me'. I believed him as I could put no limit on what he was capable of doing. He was out of control and I felt paralysed in fear that he had something else up his sleeve to try and break or destroy me. I discovered, as usual, my instincts were right. Within hours Social Services knocked on the door to see the family.

Naively, assuming this support agency were there to assist me or the children, I had hijacked my own calculation that finally someone would see through the current situation and offer insight, comprehension or support for the emotional abuse I was facing. However, Jonathan took the two young women into the kitchen and spoke to them for at least twenty minutes before they asked to speak to me alone. He led them to me full of his sophisticated charm that he could turn on like a switch, delighting the two young, inexperienced workers whose egos automatically grew as the power they held was endorsed.

Had I known my rights I would have been more prepared, but I listened like a victim as they put the world to rights and pointed a finger at me, whilst instructing as to how I should and should not behave with the children. My crime still unspoken, I gave in and said "yes" and "no" in the right places, currently too exhausted to disagree, let alone put my own defense forward. Deep in my being I felt a case had been already been written against me and I was now too drained physically and emotionally to offer an alternative view to the one already presented by my smartly dressed, confident and well-spoken husband, who always appeared so in control to all outside of home. Backed by his mother—who knew the ins and outs of social work—they had without doubt between them calculated how to have my children removed.

By contrast, I had gone from being head of an art department at one of the largest and most successful international colleges in the world, to a tired and withdrawn mother of three young children. I could barely utter a word, let alone stand up for myself. I had lost weight through my recurrent illness, and wore the burden of my marriage on my shoulders, alone and very frightened. I ached for someone to understand the isolation and loneliness, but it seemed that today was not the day. To be honest I just wanted to make it all okay for the children and was relieved when this long twenty four hours were over.

The Social Services employees wrote their notes, spoke at me what they wanted to say and left to be paid the salary they received for file filling, as opposed to embracing what was erupting as potentially a perilous situation for my children. What was presently materialising was a catastrophe of significant proportions but it was invisible to the untrained eye, and was about to roller-coaster into the destruction of my children's lives. Even I was still unaware of the horror of all that lay ahead.

CHAPTER THREE

"All right I will go," was my response to the Social Service request for a mental health assessment at the Royal Hamlet Hospital in Richmond, on that ghastly October day. As I sat in front of Sasha Mumford, I felt like I was suddenly under a Gestapo-like organisation who could dictate my every move and I submitted to their authority, too fragile to fight. In fact I called the hospital myself to speed up the process following the referral, as I assumed wrongly, that if my name was cleared, my children could soon come home. At the same time I was still unaware as to why Social Services had requested a mental health assessment, or what right they had to do so. They had not carried out any statutory 'initial assessment', nor had they completed a 'core assessment', required before intervening in the private affairs of our family. They had not revealed any concerns, not placed the children on any register nor even acknowledged they were involved with my family.

I had never suffered from any mental health issues and the only time I had ever heard the term mentioned was by my husband to me, who used it frequently in the months leading up to this time, when making accusations against me in our home. I began to wonder at this moment whether I was being set up and I felt a sense of suspicion being roused as to how much involvement he had already had with Social Services inconspicuously behind my back.

I was seen the following day by a psychiatrist whom I would describe as thorough and professional, leaving no questions off the list I was to be asked. He wrote up his report which highlighted no sign of any mental illness:

> *"She looked smartly dressed, she was appropriate, very polite, she was courteous, maintained good eye contact, her speech all through the interview which lasted an hour, was normal in flow, content and speed and there was no evidence of any type of thought disorder, there were no mannerisms of note. She exhibited no psychotic symptoms. She has no suicidal ideations or plans to harm herself or others and her insight is full."*

He highlighted how Maya was a predominant feature in our lives, over-stepping the boundaries in making major family decisions and being supported by Jonathan, which caused friction and relationship difficulties between the two of us. He emphasised how her role had reversed with mine highlighting how she interfered. He documented additionally how she gave orders which were supported by my husband, and even joined in the conversations about my 'mental illness', collaborating with my in-laws to have my children removed from me. He wrote incontestably that I suffered from the usual problems associated with a difficult marriage and the effects of my husband's unreliability due to his use of alcohol which was exacerbating the situation. It discussed my secure family history with two sisters and older parents who raised us. It acknowledged exhaustion and my physical sickness, but seemed to mention nothing of any concern that would insinuate my children were not safe in my care. The report was sent immediately to Social Services but I asked for a copy which I could take by hand that same day, not wanting the excuse for the mail system to delay my children's return.

To my dismay Social Services were not interested in the report that they had requested nor were they concerned about the absence of any mental health diagnosis. It suddenly became apparent that they were on some hidden mission working alongside my husband and were not going to deviate from the path they had chosen.

On the sixth of October 2003, day five of this ordeal, I received an A4 envelope, stamped 'Brentford County Court'. It was my thirty-ninth birthday and alone, I opened a court summons which read:

> *"Due to the continuing demise of my wife's mental health state following a diagnosis of a personality disorder and a prolonged period of emotional abuse of the children, I feel I must now protect my children by removing them from the former matrimonial home to a safe place while my wife receives treatment for her illness. In the circumstances I am applying for an interim residence order of all 3 children."*

A bomb could have landed at that moment and I would have reacted no more or no less. I felt sick to the core and my body rippled like corrugated iron in response to the shock and the disbelief that this could be real. Mentally ill? The diagnosis of a personality disorder? Abusing the children? Really?

There was a hearing lined up for November, which seemed an eternity away, as each day without the children slowed more and more. I needed a solicitor but not only had Jonathan gone, he had withdrawn all the money from our joint bank account and left me with none. I had no income of my own and we had no savings, so I had to rely on the generosity of others to get me through this time and I needed funds to be able to fight for my children's return. I had never had a legal representative before; I had never been to court and knew nothing about legal proceedings.

Worse still, I had been vomiting for the previous week and discovered that my recent increased weakness and exhaustion was not just my physical health deteriorating further, but the early signs of another pregnancy as validated by the two blue lines on the test stick I had purchased from the chemist and then had confirmed by my GP. I wondered whether loneliness could ever consume me more as I hopped on and off buses searching solicitors from the Yellow Pages, all of who confirmed they had filled their legal aid quota for the year and could not take me on.

I had not spoken of my marriage difficulties with my extended family, as so much shame was attached to its failure. I felt isolated in a bleak place that seemed to be spiralling faster than I could stay hanging on, and yet I knew instinctively I had to get my children home. So many thoughts raced through my mind as to where they were and whether they were safe and my heart bled as I imagined them crying and calling for their mother who was not answering them because I wasn't there. I wondered who would cuddle them, or feed them, or put them to bed, or get up for them in the night, or tell them that mummy loved them. We had our own quirky little routines and I pondered how they dealt with everything being so new; their home, their environment, the food they ate, the people they saw each day, the clothes they wore, the way they were bathed and even the way they were put to bed each night. Every time thoughts entered my mind, tears would stream down my cheeks as it all became too heavy a burden to bear. Yet I had to remain strong.

I had to hang on, I had to fight and I had to survive all that each day brought for the sake of these little lives that deserved the right to having their mother by their side.

My first breakthrough came with a call from Victim Support—a wonderful gentle voice on the end of the phone from someone who identified herself as Maria and offered advice. I recounted stories of endless solicitors I had visited or called, by this time twenty two in total, who had all turned me away because I had no money. I related many dismal stories of them showing me to the door unable to help, insensitive to the dilemma I faced, or rude, or abrupt, or over-busy, or worse still admitting they did not have a clue as to what I should do. More astounding was a meeting with a family lawyer in Richmond who saw me for half an hour, advised me he could not help and then invoiced me £1000 for the privilege of his time. There seemed little empathy in the world of law, but the voice presently on the end of the phone was of a lady somewhere in her sixties, who was sensitive, yet strong and highly efficient at getting straight to the point.

She wasted no time in awarding me as much information as she had acquired in her many years of supporting victims, who had been passed on to her through the police. She gave me some phone numbers and advised how I should proceed each day. She cautioned me as to what I should say, suggesting I advocate great discernment as to the choice of friends with whom I now spoke. I sensed this was an angel who had appeared in my life and I felt the relief seep from every part of my body, as finally this gentle attentive lady not only listened to my story, but heard all I had to say. I perceived she regrettably must have suffered a degree of loss at some time in her life, as otherwise she would not have been able to meet and hold me in the depths to which I had gone. I knew then and there that I was not alone. I instinctually sensed that someone with more strength than me was standing by my side and had the tenacity to not only fight for me, but be the support I needed at this time.

My two sisters joined Maria as strong warriors beside me, aiding in any way they could. Belle, my elder sister by fifteen months, lived in New Zealand but had been on the end of the phone sometimes daily through the struggles of the past year, when my husband returned home under the influence of alcohol in the early hours of the morning. She listened as I recounted endless tales of all that had taken place behind the closed doors that the world never saw. She was discerningly perceptive and understood all that had been going on and had held me so many times through the worry and uncertainty surrounding the erratic behaviour I witnessed from my husband whose conduct I could not explain. She would do all she could to fight for the return of the niece and nephews she cherished. In the near distant future she would appear in England to be at my side, leaving behind a family as well as a demanding and highly renowned career as a palliative care consultant at a large teaching hospital in Auckland.

Laura, my youngest sister by only eighteen months, was the mother of two lovely boys and portrayed a profound sense of confidence and wisdom in her ability to parent her children. This combined with her gentle, nurturing personality, ensured she supported me practically, emotionally and mentally many more times than I could ever recount. She visited our house in Twickenham and met with me on so many occasions during this period, that eventually it became easier for me to take up residence in one of her spare rooms, in her Reading detached home. She also had a young family whose needs in the midst of my situation, were not being met.

It was also becoming too much to bear the pain of seeing my children's rooms filled with their empty presence and I could not stand the hopelessness of the silence in the house, which had always been filled with such a joyful presence of their lives. The house somehow seemed frighteningly invaded with loss and I needed no more reminders of all that was missing, neither did I want to be in the geographical environment which held memories of the routines we had each day.

Laura's husband Peter could only be described as a 'rock'. He was dependable, reliable, sensitive, articulate and intelligent. He had a business intellect that could see strategy ahead and was good company to be around, as he was rational, clear minded and fun. Between the two of them they took on the great burden of responsibility bearing the same pain that I did, both of them searching for ways through the dilemma on my hands.

My father was almost eighty and had lived alone since our dear mother passed away seventeen years earlier. A devout Catholic and a true gentleman in every way, he had fought in the war in Burma and had witnessed some of the worst atrocities that the world had ever known, yet it was evident his heart broke like mine. He was a man of real integrity, truth and humility and responded by calling Jonathan and asking him to return home with the children. He communicated how as part of the marriage covenant he had taken a vow at our wedding to support us through any difficulty we would face and reminded him that his parents had done the same. He expressed a deep disapproval for their unhealthy involvement in our relationship and condemned their behaviour as destructive. He mentioned to Jonathan that he should stop listening to his mother, and he asked expectantly if he could see the children at his home for a day, but was told in response, "You are not a fit man to have my children."

To my father's great credit and in honour of all he believed, he never once to the day he died discredited the children's father verbally or otherwise, not even through all that Jonathan was later to do. I knew in him was rooted a strong generational heritage of love; a quiet, kind, gentle, patient, forgiving and enduring love. In witnessing the way he handled all that would unravel, I perceived he had somehow exposed my children to a personal gift of all that he would leave behind, as an inheritance and legacy from one who stood the test of the greatest of trials that one could throw at a man.

My second breakthrough came following one of the last solicitor's calls I made through the Yellow Pages, and the conversation with an engaging and very accommodating young lady with whom I spoke. She informed me I should not be looking for a family solicitor but a child abduction lawyer, and recommended Emily Hewlett OBE in the city, who worked with snatched and kidnapped children. I called her instantly. She agreed to take me on after I had met her in her London office and she had established that I could be accepted on legal aid if I was eligible for income support. I had no idea about legal aid other than it would pay my fees and nor was I aware that I could claim income support, finding myself in a situation where I qualified for money from the government to meet my living costs. So far I had survived only on food given by neighbours or money donated by the local church. I immediately 'signed on' at the local job centre and Emily sent someone to represent me in court.

The hearing was scheduled for only a few days later which had cut it quite fine, but on arrival at court we discovered it was set down only for five minutes, as my husband's legal team had assumed it would be just a quick tick in a box. The judge however, on reading the evidence, decided a longer session was needed as the prosecution had produced a diagnosis of mental illness to the court, and the time allocated was not sufficient to see the hearing through.

It was six weeks since I had seen my children and it took that long to discover they were living with my in-laws in Dorset. Not only had Social Services refused to identify their location, but Jonathan had also been advised to not let me know of the children's whereabouts. He had not only housed them with his parents and Maya, but had started Harry at the local school. Annie had been placed in a nursery nearby, while he travelled overseas and commuted into London from their house when he was around. My heart, if not broken into enough pieces already, broke twice more, once for the knowledge of where they were living and again for the awareness that I would have to wait another 3 weeks until the next court hearing. Meanwhile the judge awarded me an hour's access once a week at a neutral meeting point to see my children.

I left the court and broke down.

CHAPTER FOUR

It was heart wrenching to be told I was allowed to see my children only on supervised visits, when I had cared for them almost single handedly for the previous five years while Jonathan travelled for long periods of time. No one had ever questioned my ability to love or care for any of the children. There was no evidence documented of abandonment, abuse or neglect, no concerns shown by schools, health visitors, doctors, friends or relatives. Yet an order was passed which meant I was only allowed to see them whilst being watched and observed by adults, whom I later discovered would report back to Social Services all they saw.

Before my first trip and at a time when Jonathan still denied me access, my sister Laura had visited them in Dorset. I had given her Harry's teddy to pass to him with a message that it was from his mummy and filled with all her love for him. His little heart-wrenching response was, "I know it's not from my Mummy because my Mummy is dead. If she wasn't she would have brought teddy herself." They were words that would be replayed many times in my mind in the months and years to come, like a record that had got stuck on one of its grooves and would only repeat a single sound. I recognised that something in Harry had died and had been replaced by the awareness that his little internal world was no longer safe. All I had secured in him over the past few years had been ripped out and the innocence of a protected childhood had gone. I feared this would mean he would never be the same, happy, confident little boy ever again and the childhood I had so hoped to give my children was never going to be.

It meant a lot therefore that I would be able to reassure Harry by seeing him in person, but I still struggled with the affect it would have on the three of them. I wasn't sure how to feel because although elated that I would finally get to hold them and show them I was still alive, I worried about the impact it would have on the trauma that they would be experiencing.

My mind was suggesting that if they were going to be returned in three weeks through the court, it would be better and less disturbing for them not to see me, rather than us be together for an hour and then have me walk away, as though I didn't care or didn't want them, reinforcing the rejection they already felt. They were too young to understand anything other than their need for their mother and I didn't want to be in a situation where I was seemingly abandoning them. They were not of an age where I could explain what was going on, other than to reassure them that I loved them very much and we would be back together soon.

I sought the advice of a paediatrician who warned me that the children would present as traumatised and would react in different ways. She said that Alfred aged one would respond as though I had died and would be in a place of deep loss and grief and would reject me if he saw me. Could I then see him and walk away? I decided that I couldn't, as it would be better for the children to wait and just bring them home in a few weeks' time. Social Services however, had other ideas and communicated to me that I would follow only what they instructed. They told me I had to go or I would get a bad report from them to the court saying I was not interested in the well-being of my children.

Accordingly I hired a car with borrowed money and drove to where Jonathan agreed I could meet. I took two trains and a bus to get to the cheapest car hire I could find in Reading and stopped regularly as I drove, vomiting on the motorway's hard shoulder as early pregnancy took its toll. My wonderful father accompanied me. Now quite elderly, he supported me in every way he could, whilst bearing the visible scars of an internal burden of worry and concern for the grandchildren he adored. I had been told that I could meet the children in the house of a relative of my husband's in Portsmouth and that I should text him as I came off the motorway to find the address. We duly arrived and stopped the car to find which route to take, but the response was not one I had expected:

"Sorry, I have decided it is not safe for the children to see you so we have not come to Portsmouth today."

It was eleven in the morning and I had left home four hours earlier so as to not be late. I turned around and there were simply no words to describe our journey home as I cried so many tears that not even windscreen wipers would have cleared my vision. I couldn't see the road, or hard shoulders, I didn't know which way I was going and my whole body was so fragile it was even hard to keep hold of the wheel.

The second arrangement to see the children was seven days later when Jonathan organised for me to meet them in a park in Salisbury. I repeated the car hire and vomiting procedure and arrived with the children in view. True to the doctor's words, Alfred rejected me and clung to his father's hip whilst Harry and Annie ran up shouting and screaming, 'Mummy', and never left my side. I took Alfred and cuddled him and hugged him whilst he sat on my lap lost, as though in another place. My adorable one year old blond had in a few weeks disappeared from a giggling, mischievous, strong willed, determined child to a toddler that looked like he was disturbed from the effects of a holocaust. He was withdrawn, sullen, grey in colour and gaunt. The boy I knew so well had vanished into another realm. Instead of feeling a bond and connection between us, I picked up only pain. Deep profound pain; confusion, hurt, anger and a disorientation that manifested as an absent and misplaced child.

Annie and Harry played and hugged me, and were so excited that the parting after only an hour of playing on the swings, hide and seek and talking, hit them suddenly in a harrowing and agonizing way. They clung to my legs as I held Alfred, begging and pleading for me not to go and insisting they come home with me. They screamed, they kicked, they gave all they could in a lost attempt to remain with the only person who had been with them all their lives. Rejecting one's children goes against anything and everything a mother is ever made to be, but as Jonathan called the children, and I knew all would be reported back to court, I had to peel them off my legs as he stood and watched us all. I struggled as I had to push them to their father and as I turned my back on them and walked to the car all I could hear were their piercing screams that would ring in my ears for days to come. I thought of a scene in the concentration camps where children were ripped away from their mothers as they disembarked trains and I understood for the first time the injustice, the suffering and the pain of the forced separation that the children must have endured in those moments.

For the third arrangement in the six week period I was told to meet at another cousin's house. The days leading up to it reinforced the fear of an repeat situation for the children and I, but Social Services were on my back not only dictating my every move, but watching my every response. I duly obeyed, and arrived to the same greeting by the two older children at the address I had been given. I resentfully noticed the new clothes they were wearing that grandma had bought and they showed me their recently acquired toys that bribed them into an unfamiliar way of life.

Alfred would not come to me and I could not add to his distress. He clung tightly to his father, but was not even secure there, he could not smile and his pain pierced me to the core. His hair had been heartlessly cut by his grandmother and the crooked, cropped fringe was a representation serving only to epitomize the brutality of all he had endured since he had been taken. Nothing I could write and no dictionary words could describe the helplessness I felt as his mother being unable to meet his needs. Alfred's basic human rights had been violated and this would be deeply buried within him and come back in later life to disturb him and haunt him, niggling away at everything he would ever set out to do.

Annie was a little girl of three and needed so desperately to come home. She longed for me and pleaded with me and tried with such courage to be strong and brave, as she fought away the tears of again seeing me and not being allowed to come back to all she knew as familiar and secure. She simply could not understand all that was being explained to her, as in her mind it was wrong. In her little 'Annie world' she loved me and needed me and that's all that she could know. How then could she understand something so incongruous as her father telling her she could not come home when she was with me right now?

Harry too was brave and strong, fighting away all his anger, trying not to acknowledge his own needs. At aged only five he was responding almost as an adult boy, selflessly looking out for the requirements of his siblings, protecting them and telling me he would look after them whilst I was not around. He busied himself with any toy he could find and pushed me away with such resolution, knowing that a hug would break him and not make him the man he suddenly had to be.

Jonathan's cousin called out to say that lunch was ready and they all ate with the children whilst I waited in the living room, my time nearly up and fear gripping me for tomorrow was the day in court that would determine the future of all our lives. I felt my insides being ripped out and wondered if they could survive being done so again, and then I discovered I was bleeding. Panic set in, I had lost my children and now worried that all the emotion I carried would mean that I would maybe lose my baby. Jonathan by this stage knew of my pregnancy, but he had said nothing other than announcing in a letter that his mother thought I was lying. She said I was using it as an excuse to get my husband back, indicating it was further evidence of my mental ill health. I told him at this moment that I was bleeding but received no response. He said nothing and expressed no words regarding the fact I was possibly losing our fourth child. All I saw was another blank empty glance and he watched while I walked to the car with no other choice of where to go.

Realising I would not make it home in the condition I was in, I remembered an aunt and uncle of my husband's who lived in the area and decided I would call in so I could stop for a rest. They were kind people and I felt a bond with them as they had accepted me and welcomed me into their family from the minute we first met seven years earlier. We had a lovely relaxed relationship as they were fun, hospitable and gentle in nature. I knocked on the door and luckily they were in. I explained that I had just seen the children and was in need of a cup of tea because I was worried that I might be losing the baby. I knew they would embrace me and be non-judgmental, that they would understand and would listen, but I had assumed wrongly. The final straw in yet another dreadful day was their harsh and severe response, informing me that I was not welcome, as they escorted me to my car. Obviously they were in a difficult situation but I was stunned. My family still cared for Jonathan and had not taken sides, wishing to support us both through the difficulties in our marriage, but here was the hostility in his family I faced, that was to never go away.

Shocked, I left and as I drove I cried tears that burnt as they rolled down my cheeks. The salty streams came like waterfalls annoyingly bursting and forcing their way out, and for all the times I had tried to remain strong I could not now. My children were gone. They longed to come home and I could do nothing to meet their needs. I faced court the next day and not only had the family I married into all turned their backs on me, but I feared I was additionally losing my baby. I was facing it all alone with the realisation that the man I longed to be supporting me, standing by my side, the one I had taken my vows to remain with forever, was indeed the very man who had initiated all that was going on at this time.

I had to drive but couldn't. I drove on some road going somewhere and knew I was a danger in the traffic, as I couldn't see physically or emotionally which way I was going. I pulled in at a petrol station and broke down. The shock, the anger, the pain, the loss, the grief, the hurt, the rejection, the fear, the injustice, the cruelty and the suffering I witnessed on my children's faces all came out in my tears. I broke and I knew of no other way. It was no longer something I could contain and regardless of who was filling up with petrol or what was around, I sobbed in a way I never knew possible and out it all came. I was so utterly isolated as it seemed all hope had gone and I knew I was too weak and weary to even fight for the return of my children.

An hour passed and then another and in the petrol station I remained as the world went by. Not knowing the time or where I was, exhausted and drained I sat in that empty space until it was dark and somehow on autopilot the hired car got me home.

CHAPTER FIVE

I was early arriving in Brentford County Court, having already met my younger sister who was there to accompany me for the day. We entered a 1970's horrible tacky hotel for a breakfast that neither she nor I could eat, ordered a cup of tea that was the last thing we really wanted and fiddled with the spoons on the saucers, unable to even drink what had been placed in front of us. We then made our way to where the case was to be held and immediately saw that the court could not have been more formidable. It was an ugly, grey stone, concrete building which seemed to fit perfectly into its run down, depressed, degenerated and bedraggled surroundings and reflected deeply the mood of the day.

Inside the blue carpets smelt of decay and neglect and served to remind me of all I knew my children were experiencing, having already read the reports of the local health visitor in Dorset. She had recounted that the children were showing great signs of distress, were bed wetting and having repeated nightmares. She wrote of children crying for their mother and the effects from being confused, withdrawn and disturbed.

'What if?' was the only question on my mind. The obvious decision for any judge was to bring Harry, Annie and Alfred home. I cherished my children, had never harmed them, was not mentally ill and my husband had taken them, or, rather abducted them, with Social Services supposedly backing him. Furthermore there was no evidence or writing to show that they had carried out any formal investigation into the family dynamics, or the health, safety or welfare of our children.

My legal team submitted evidence from the nursery, the school and our family GP that were only supportive of the children coming home. The judge heard how the psychiatrist 'to whom the mother was referred by social services', found no mental abnormality of any kind whatsoever. He heard the description from the principal of the nursery school which said:

> *"Annie's relationship with her mother Lily is one of warmth as they delight in each other's company."*

He listened to the writing from the general practitioner:

> *"Having discussed the matter with other members of the practice, who have been involved in the mother's care, I find no concerns whatsoever of myself, my colleagues or the health visitor regarding the mother's ability to care for the children."*

Yet fear set in. Jonathan had been seeing a psychiatrist named Dr Andrew Harwell who worked in private practice and through his work with Jonathan, had diagnosed me with Borderline Personality Disorder (BPD). He had called me to ask for help with the treatment of Jonathan and in doing so wrote a report on me, even though I was never in a client relationship with him and never met with him as a patient. Later we discovered he was someone that was well known to my mother-in-law through her previous work with Social Services and I sensed that he had been involved by the family to unethically diagnose me, through my husband meeting with him regularly.

Not only was Dr Harwell's diagnosis forwarded without my knowledge to Social Services, but Jonathan was also using it as evidence in court. In front of us we now had papers where Dr Harwell wrote broadly about a typical patient. He used speech that implied he was speaking about me but did not use my name, nor did he explain why I might fit into this category:

> *"I would say it is a common feature in people with Borderline Personality Disorder for them to make repeated threats of suicide. Sometimes suicide is attempted and of course on occasions it is completed successfully. All children are seen as an extension of the individual's persona and psyche, then, the distorted suicidal thinking extends to not abandoning children, because of fear of abandonment is one of the most powerful drives of this type of person. Therefore a parent in these circumstances can only commit suicide and not abandon their children if they also kill their children."*

Accompanying his writing was a copied eight page document of how 'a typical BPD type' might present. Furthermore this exhaustive list detailed:

"They usually have a self-image based on being bad or evil and display impulsivity in at least two areas that are self-damaging. They may gamble, spend money irresponsibly, binge eat, abuse substances, engage in un-safe sex, or drive recklessly. Individuals with BPD display recurrent suicidal behaviour, gestures or threats, or self-mutilating behaviour. Self-mutilative acts (e.g. cutting or burning) are very common. Undermining themselves at the moment a goal is about to be realised is common e.g. dropping out of school. Some develop psychotic-like symptoms e.g. hallucinations, body-image distortions, ideas of reference and hypnagogic phenomena. Individuals with this disorder may feel more at home with a pet or inanimate possession. Physical handicaps may result from inflicted abuse behaviours or failed suicide attempts. Physical and sexual abuse, neglect and hostile conflict are more common in early childhood histories. Common co-occurring Axis 1 disorders include Mood Disorders, Substance-Related Disorders, Eating Disorders and Attention-Deficit Hyperactivity Disorder."

The long list went on to include identity disturbance, impulsivity and other related personality disorders.

I read the report before me aghast at what had been presented; having never self-harmed or suffered from eating disorders. I had never been abused sexually or physically as a child, never attempted suicide, never self-mutilated, never spent money irresponsibly or gambled, never abused substances, had never kept pets, never dropped out of school or a career. I had not thought of myself as 'evil' and certainly wasn't physically handicapped from inflicted abuse. I had been told by the psychiatrist that I displayed no psychotic-like symptoms or any other form of mental illness. In fact none of any of his listed 'attachments' identified me, my behaviour or my past.

Neither did his writing refer to 'me', or identify how evidence of any of the above displayed in me. He had submitted a report to the court written about a 'typical' personality who would have this type of disorder and I was concerned he might have added reports on all sorts of mental illness, behaviour patterns and disorders, because they would have been as irrelevant as the so called 'evidence' he had produced.

I feared how the judge was to respond to this report. He didn't know me from Adam. He knew nothing of my background, my personality, my history, relationships, mannerisms, behaviour et cetera. Yet here was a report detailing how I should 'present' because I was supposed to have a Borderline Personality Disorder, diagnosed by a man who was my husband's psychiatrist! It seemed impossible at this moment that the evidence presented could be any more surreal, incongruous, bizarre, contradictory, incoherent or conflicting. Factual evidence to have my children removed from me was surely not going to be based on this?

Social Services were a professional body who were meant to operate to protect my children but they had failed. My husband's treating psychiatrist had unethically diagnosed me with a mental illness and I worried that the court would somehow be deceived and get it all horribly wrong. My sister and I both felt anxiety reawaken as we were led to the same room we had been in only a few weeks earlier, it had an oppressive feel of misrepresentation and distortion the minute one walked in.

I met my barrister Charles, a highly respected, well presented man who could not have been kinder or more astute. He explained the procedure and was sensitive as he picked up on my vulnerability and nervousness, stepping in and reassuring me at a time I felt I had very little confidence left and we went into court to persuade the judge to bring the children home.

Judge Oppelt sat there as I expected, peering through his glasses looking at me and then at Jonathan trying to sum up in his mind from first impressions what was going on in both of our lives. He looked at me intently and then away. He listened as both sides presented their case for removing or keeping the children. It was as though there was an important tennis match going on and the one who hit the ball the hardest would win each point and then the ultimate game, set and match. The outcome of my children's lives was currently down to an activity being undertaken between two people who knew nothing about them, had never met them and whatever happened were going to make a good living out of the sport they had chosen as a career. Worse still the umpire who kept score and called for the rallies, was going to base his decision on what people were saying about me, yet had never witnessed me raising my children. How was this man wearing a wig in any position to decide what might be best for the children I had carried and delivered into this world and how was he to ever know of the truth of what really had been going on in the family home?

The judge listened to Dr Harwell's report diagnosing Borderline Personality Disorder and my insides churned like butter being made into cream. As I sat, I listened to my husband request that I should be admitted to the Cassel Hospital in Ham for psychiatric treatment under a Dr Kimberly, as recommended by Dr Harwell. My husband wanted me sectioned!

I weighed up my impressions of the judge, who seemed amiable and I noted a tame smile that occasionally tried to emerge from the corner of his mouth and I read it incorrectly as compassion and believed that all would be in order. We adjourned after the evidence had been given and were called back in for his summing up and final decision.

He spoke with authority describing how the children had been taken away from their mother and the only home and security that they had ever known. He said that it went against human rights to remove the children so abruptly from their routine and all that was familiar, which included the daily visits from the family milkman, relationships with friends they loved and the safety they experienced in the local environment which was an important part of their lives. He summarised by saying that the children were showing great signs of distress where they were staying with grandparents. He described how they hadn't only lost their mother, but were not even in the care of their father, as he travelled away and did not see them most days, and took to heart the distress described by their new health visitor. He also said that the report produced by Dr Harwell was not reliable evidence as my husband had been his client rather than me. He then read out an email my mother-in-law had written to Dr Harwell suggesting that her son was not even a hundred per cent certain of what he was doing:

> *"We are witnessing Jonathan's inability to put the children's needs first."*
> *"Jonathan is racked with guilt about taking the children away from their mother."*
> *"Jonathan says she is a good mother."*
> *"Social Services seem unwilling to give credence to your diagnosis."*
> *"Jonathan himself may well require psychiatric treatment."*

The judge encouragingly went on to highlight that by my own submissions and the evidence from the local authority report it was clear I was not mentally ill, neither was there was any evidence to show the children were being harmed in my care. I felt a small warmth and thrill creep inside and sensed the birthing of a tiny smile on my face which was materialising but could not quite surface.

Then he spoke his final words summing up to say that the children had been gone for six weeks and he did not want to unsettle them once more and change the status quo. He awarded the interim residence order to the father and requested a full hearing at a future date to be set at the end of February, in three months time. Furthermore he requested that the whole family be seen by Dr Kimberly at the Cassel Hospital in Ham.

I had lost my children and could not get them home. My husband had succeeded in taking the children from me with a penal order attached and furthermore Dr Harwell's recommendation that I be seen by Dr Kimberly was accepted and written into the order. I was without my children on a long term basis and there was no one to protect them. I bled again heavily and my sister drove me away.

CHAPTER SIX

She drove me back to her home via the hospital, knowing I could no longer return to Twickenham alone and probably aware that I would not survive another night without the emotional support of someone beside me to see me through.

I could not speak. I could not eat. I was utterly numb with disbelief. Shock tore through my weak body, ripping it further into shreds that could no longer hold together. I felt mutilated by the torment of not having properly cuddled my children for so long and hearing of their suffering through the court. I was now like a robot, just going through the motions. I had a scan which told me the baby was still there but how could that mean anything at all when I was so totally absent? I had disappeared into a distant place of pain and could not come out. I sat in the kitchen and the agony ate away at me like a mouse with fresh cheese, holes appeared in

CHAPTER SIX

places of my inner being that I thought had already gone and my mind was going into deep dark places.

Thoughts raced around my head. Had I abused my children? Was I mentally ill? If I hadn't and if I wasn't, what had I done to deserve all this? How could I lose my children in an English judicial system that was supposedly honest and fair? The thought of what Harry, Annie and Alfred were going through was worse still, as was the knowledge that I could not be there for them as they cried for comfort in the nights when they woke, nor explain my love to each of them. All I wanted was to just hold them and absorb some of their anguish and confusion and feel it drain from their tiny bodies, still so very young.

Night time brought darkness which was not blacker than the place I was already in, and I lay alone in an empty bed longing for a deep sleep to take me, as there seemed no hope to remain awake for. I just lay there for what seemed like an eternity too distraught to even move from the horizontal position gripping the pillow soaked in my tears. I had lost everything. Memories of all the past nights haunted me and I was uncertain how I could manage another. The thought of the children suffering so badly and not being able to rescue them, protect them or comfort them was simply more than I was able to comprehend. The days were bad enough but the nights were excessively long and exorbitantly painful. My whole body ached intensely, and there were no tablets or remedies that could heal or numb it. On and on it went and the tears kept surging from an ever increasing supply that seemed unable to end.

The days went on and my sister was wonderful; loving and gentle, understanding, strong and patient. She was broken as well, at my loss and the children's suffering, but she carried on supporting me through what she also experienced as wrong. Peter, a rock as always, must have sensed a need to speak and came in when nothing more could be said and sat me up, insisting I listen. He spoke forcefully with unyielding strength and tenacity. He voiced what he described as the truth—releasing one final bit of strength that allowed me to breathe another breath that I did not wish to even inhale. His timing was perfect and he must have known I needed just one ray of hope to take me through the next minutes, as the place I was in was so black I could see nothing ahead and I needed the knowledge that someone else could.

In fact he spoke not to me, knowing I probably would not hear, but at me telling me I was not mentally ill, nor had I harmed my children. He explained how my children needed me and that I was not about to give up or give in to some pathetic judge in court who had made a wrong decision and allow myself to accept he was right. He told me I was to fight for them, for little Annie who so needed her mother, for Alfred who should be sitting in my arms and for Harry who with his siblings had faced a grave injustice and needed to return home. He said I had to fight for the baby inside me that deserved a chance, not only at life, but who also had the right to be with, and be raised alongside its brothers and sister. He articulated there would be a way forward but if I gave up the children would grow without the very person they needed in life to heal them and pull them through.

He was right. I knew he was right. Every word he uttered made sense and I hung on in my mind to his strength and determination for me. Too despondent to even utter a word I thanked him from a place of silence for being a rock and an anchor, and for being the hope I needed at the very bottom of my pit. The hope wasn't huge, as I still couldn't see a way through, but at least as small as it was, it became the foothold to carry on at least another few moments. I had to find some way of gaining enough strength to battle for the rights of my children. If the system was going to fail them so badly, I wasn't going to stand on the same side and walk away. I was going to rise up and fight for them. Falling apart was the very last thing they needed me to do.

I continued to stay at my sister's house eating what I could and watching her children come and go as normal conversations were had, which became a welcome distraction from the repercussion of the past few days. I did not return to the family home and could not bear to see anything that would remind me of my children more than my thoughts insisted on doing. It was as though I was on a ghost train continually entering a haunted house, unable to get off or come back outside.

CHAPTER SEVEN

As the days progressed, at last there was a welcome and unexpected call from my solicitor. Emily Hewlett was on the line and it was a relief to hear her voice, as it embodied a connection with someone who was able to professionally critique the ruling that had been made in court and assess the way forward. The absence of her presence on the end of the phone line in the past few days had imposed an acute resonance of an 'ending' to the proceedings and an abandonment into accepting the transition from motherhood into a single life of loss. Suddenly however, her voice instilled hope and I knew she was the only one who would know the way to proceed. It was also a comfort to ascertain that I was not alone in feeling the injustice. She was angry and it was reassuring to know that those fighting on my behalf were outraged enough to not walk away. I took great reassurance in listening to her negative appraisal of the hearing, criticising the decision that had been made. She drew attention to the alarm bells that had been ringing in my ears which were: Why did the judge summarise to return the children home but not do so?

Something in me stirred as I heard the Court of Appeal mentioned, but frustration presented like an encore as she discussed how we could not get there as my funding had ended. I was claiming legal aid and it had been limited to the last hearing and it would take another lengthy application to apply for more, with not even the assurance that I would be successful.

The sudden hope and then the loss became a roller coaster ride which awoke me abruptly as though from a deep sleep. Like a warrior I prepared for battle; took hold of my armour and was ready to fight to get the funding. If nothing else I was aroused sufficiently with a new vehemence to be able to fight for the return of my children. Social Services, Doctor Harwell and the court were one thing, so far I had lost to all three, but I was not going to lose the battle because of funding.

It took a few weeks, but the funding allocation did eventually come through, closely followed by a date for a hearing at the Court of Appeal. December the eighteenth rang in my ears as I counted the days and thought of my beautiful children, hoping they could bravely hang on for a little longer. It had been sixty six days since they had been taken from home and even another twelve days seemed an unbelievable length of time to wait, as I continued to wonder what they had been told and whether they feared they would never see me again.

My sister Belle made the decision that back up was needed and she found a locum to replace her at work. She flew over from New Zealand and arrived determined she would not depart again until my children had returned. Her strength alongside that of Laura and Peter and my wonderful friends, who had been by my side thus far, was to be the crutch I needed to hold me up and see me through what lay ahead as I remained unaware of the emotional mountains I still had to climb.

Maria from Victim Support meanwhile had become like a mother, calling, phoning and meeting me, encouraging me and guiding me with each step I took. Although my dependence on those around me at this time was draining, the love shared by those close to me meant so much. More importantly still, being surrounded by people who believed in me became the adrenalin I needed. It enabled me to continue to fight.

By this stage, A4 envelopes were arriving fast and furious through the front door of my home in Twickenham where I had returned for a few days at a time, like a baby slowly being weaned onto solid food. Every morning the packages arrived, each one getting fatter and fatter, revealing the obesity of the motivation running this persistently incongruous case. My husband was presently gathering evidence with hurried relentlessness as he submitted testimonies from his mother, his brother, his boss at work and Maya, who was currently taking care of my children alongside my in-laws. As he had no evidence to prove I was either mentally ill or abusing the children, he was having to rely on anything he could find from what family and friends said about me or from information he could gather from my past. He had a severe obsession and was a man on a mission; nothing was to stop him whether it was ethical, moral or fair.

I received knocks on the door from friends who said Jonathan had asked them to give evidence in court and they had replied asking what on earth they were to say, as they had seen nothing other than happy children and my love for them in the home. Statements from his mother testified that I used her to babysit whilst my friends were in the house and I would chat to them and ignore her. In reality my intention had been to introduce her to my friends and include her in my life. What this was supposed to prove I was unsure but she went on to say I was clearly mentally ill. In the early days of our marriage she had even suggested to Jonathan that I had been sexually abused by my father and I felt that what she wrote now was no less severe. She described how I was always tired when pregnant and would disappear rudely to feed a baby, rather than stay in the room with everyone else. She even documented that I had eating problems, as she thought I was always ill or too thin (a typical consequence of malabsorption as a result of my undiagnosed coeliac disease). She used this to imply I was anorexic; one of the symptoms for Borderline Personality Disorder that she wanted confirmed.

As if the submissions from Jonathan's mother were not enough, Jonathan's brother with whom I thought I got on well and had been extremely fond of, helped produce a thick folder called 'The Blue File', which was an A4 ring binder based on my life. The two of them had read a book called *Treading on Eggshells* and had written me in to every single chapter, slotting me in to each personality trait documented, so that I reflected a typical Borderline Personality Disorder disposition. There was an introduction and list of contents. It gave an account of the ten personality traits which included; chronic feelings of emptiness, emotional instability, inappropriate anger, eating disorders, efforts to avoid abandonment, unstable relationships and identity disturbance. I read the list of symptoms and I wondered if they could also resemble the personality of a depressed young mother, or a woman married to an alcoholic living a life of fear.

There was a chapter on how Harry aged five (who was later to be diagnosed with classic dyslexia), could barely read or write. Examples of his handwriting were copied to prove he was being emotionally abused by his mother, as it was not as developed as it should have been for an average child of his age. Copies of pages from children's stories were added to prove that if Harry had a less abusive mother he would be reading to a higher level.

There were photos of Harry and Annie with Maya cuddling them, to prove that she was their chosen mother figure as opposed to me. Private emails I had sent for the previous few years were all copied and reproduced. Love letters to my husband were used to demonstrate I was excessively emotional or needy. Every personal detail of my life was used and twisted into something to prove Borderline Personality Disorder. The folder contained endless divided sections based on my life, my friends, family, career, behaviour, mannerisms, habits, successes, failures, abilities and idiosyncrasies all slotted in to the relevant category. They were to prove I was; underweight, overweight, withdrawn, extrovert, showing separation anxiety or dependence, rejection, despair, panic, confusion, too generous or too penurious, unstable or intense, showed identity disturbance, was impulsive, reckless, self-mutilating, bored or over-active, paranoid, filled with shame and guilt, idealizing, devaluing, paranoid or disassociating.

The 'Blue File' was enough work to submit for a university PhD on psychiatry and a thesis in itself. It portrayed a disturbing insight into the mission my husband was on to destroy me. The shock of its appearance was so severe that I had to force myself to separate from the 'content' and try and see the truth—what kind of husband would produce this type of manual on his wife, bound and duplicated with copies sent to Social Services, lawyers and the court and what would his motivation be?

All that came to mind was *Silence of the Lambs*, a taut, suspenseful, psychological thriller, where director Jonathan Demme superbly crafted a harrowing film that was dark, moody, sombre and truly frightening. In it Clarice Starling talked to Hannibal Lecter, a very powerful and clever-minded manipulator, in an attempt to gain a better insight into the twisted mind of a serial psychopathic killer. I suddenly wished that Clarice was with me, to help get into the mind of the man who chose to marry me, because I, for sure, was not able to do so.

His letters to my solicitor made it clear that he wanted me sectioned. If I could simply get the help that was needed, he would return the children and we could be happy as a family once again! He was desperate to prove he loved me, and he repeated it in support of his reasons for pursuing his current line of attack. As this dubious display of love showed, he was clearly at present a very troubled man and his attempts to publicly destroy me, as my father described, were in fact only evidence of the power and control he had previously used as tools to dominate me and discipline me within our marriage.

Further in-depth reports arrived from Dr Harwell about Borderline Personality Disorder, describing how a typical patient might present, where he copied extracts from books and medical journals. Transcripts began appearing of conversations I had been having with Jonathan over the past few weeks where he had documented word for word what I had said to him on the phone. It suddenly dawned on me why he always had to call me back if I had been the one to initiate the call. I was shocked to realise that my husband was journaling every communication between the two of us. As similar conversations appeared on paper between girlfriends of mine and Jonathan, I realised with surprise he was meeting with them and recording as he interviewed, documenting their opinions about me and the life I led.

I was sent letters from his solicitor requesting permission to access my medical records, and notes from hospitals too. My whole life was being researched, dissected, analysed and diagnosed, by what seemed to be a man fixated on sifting through everything private and personal to me with a magnifying glass, in the hopes of finding evidence that would mean the children's permanent removal from my care.

I began to panic each time the postman turned up, fearing what I was to read next. I became paranoid about hearing the letterbox clatter, as by now the files were stacking up, as his so-called evidence poured in. At the same time a jigsaw of previous events was being put together, bringing explanations to unanswered questions that were highlighted in my mind. Letters arrived that recorded communication between various combinations of my mother-in-law, father-in-law, husband, Dr Harwell and Social Services.

Dates reaching back to a year before he left with the children revealed that behind my back my husband's family had been meeting with various professionals and plotting a campaign to remove the children from me. Many letters and emails were copied in files, one of which, from my father-in-law to Dr Harwell, read as follows:

Dear Andrew,

I am writing to thank you for the time you spent with my wife, Jonathan and me last Friday. I believe that the following is a fair summary of the points we covered:

- *You confirmed your diagnosis of Lily's illness (Borderline Personality Disorder) and that her condition is at the extreme end of the spectrum.*
- *You recommend that Jonathan write to all professionals involved informing them of your diagnosis.*
- *You confirmed you are willing to talk to the Social Services team to explain your analysis of the risks to the children associated with Lily's mental illness.*
- *It is your opinion that Lily should be excluded from Jonathan's and the children's lives while she undergoes in-patient psychiatric treatment. The risks to the children are significant and they should not live in the damaging environment that exists today.*
- *You recommend that Lily be referred for assessment*

to Dr Kimberly of The Cassel Hospital in Ham. Dr Kimberly is a leading specialist in the treatment of BPD.

- *You stressed that treatment for Lily is the only route that can possibly maintain the integrity of the family and release all of its members, especially Lily from the horrible consequence of her illness.*
- *You stressed that all professionals have a duty to address the child protection issues that it contains.*
- *You recommend that Jonathan obtain appropriate legal advice from a lawyer experienced in both mental health and family law and would try to recommend a suitable person.*
- *If Lily refuses to co-operate and does not engage in an appropriate course of treatment, you recommend that Jonathan should seek an interim residence order for the children.*

The Social Services team should contact you within the next week or so. If they do not, we would ask that you write to them, as a duty of care to express your understanding of the risks to the children. We would be pleased to cover your costs for this service (contact details are attached).

Yours Sincerely,
Michael O'Shea
cc: Social Services, Jonathan O'Shea

I had sensed all along that I had been involved in a 'set-up' and here in front of me was the evidence. It proved that not only had my in-laws been organising meetings with this psychiatrist in private practice, but they were also paying him to forward his reports to

Social Services! They were the key players in both attempting to get me diagnosed and in involving Social Services. It became startlingly clear from this letter that the next stage was to get me to The Cassel Hospital in Ham.

My mind raced back to times where Jonathan acted strangely. I maybe wrongly suspected he was seeing another woman, because he was being dishonest about where he had been or who he had been talking to and lying to cover up the deviousness of his conduct. Through having Jonathan as his patient, Dr Harwell had diagnosed me with BPD and his mother had been instrumental in introducing the two of them through working with him as a colleague.

The irony of it all was that the accusation against me of mental illness and emotional harm to my children, meant all I was allowed to do was prove my innocence. As a result of being the 'respondent' I was not allowed to present a case against my husband and mention the abuse I suffered through his use of alcohol or his corresponding behaviour. This ferocious pursuit was nothing to do with the children or their emotional well-being, but about controlling me by using power and money to destroy everything I was.

CHAPTER EIGHT

The eighteenth of December arrived and I stood outside the Royal Courts of Justice, a commandingly large, grey stone, Victorian Gothic edifice built in the 1870s and opened by Queen Victoria in 1882. Commonly called the Law Courts, they house both the High Court and the Court of Appeal and include several towers, more than 1000 rooms and ornate furnishings and decorations.

These were the law courts where often journalists were seen on television; the backdrop of steps leading up to the austere yet distinctly most British of all London institutions, microphone in hand, interviewing a barrister or solicitor who had won or lost some prestigious case. It was a place where verdicts of innocence or guilt were rendered and lives were changed forever. It was disturbingly overwhelming therefore to look up and acknowledge I was to walk through those imposing doors and another judge would decide the fate of my children once and for all.

Now I was here, I felt like a criminal. A case had been brought against me and maybe I was naive in believing I was innocent. Yet at the same time it struck me once again that I had been sucked into a system of professionals who, in my limited experience, appeared more interested in protecting their salaries, position and reputation than the people in their care.

More terrifying than anything, was knowing that not one of the people I was to meet today, would ever have seen a photograph of my children let alone had met them, or witnessed the relationship we shared. No one would know how I cared for them, played with them for hours on end, pushed them on swings, fed the ducks with them, or got up in the small hours of the morning as they teethed, how I changed nappies or held my children as they fought fevers. I felt no one would understand the bond between me and my children that could cause such pain of separation unless they had suffered the same injustice. A laceration had been cut right through to the centre of my very being, caused by a primal instinct to protect Harry, Annie and Alfred as I was being denied the right to shield and safeguard my children.

I met my barrister in a small side room outside the court; a well-known counsel in family law and highly experienced in child abduction. He was stern and spoke with clarity and authority. I liked him immediately and felt safe as he knew my life as well as the numerous files inside out. He knew dates, places, names, meetings, events, conversations, accusations, investigations, assessments and could instantly turn to a page, most highlighted with coloured markers, to access information or important details for the day. I wondered how many hours he had put into reading and memorising the key facts he would use to present his case.

Before we had even stepped foot in the court I noticed how he summarised Dr Harwell well and spoke out against Judge Oppelt, to me suggesting he had been wrong in removing my children in

November. He briefed me on what would be expected once inside the room; I replied to him by saying 'yes' in the right places and 'no' as appropriate, and he advised me on how the day would unfold. We consequently filed into court and I sat dazed at the formality of the setting, with varying people allocated to different rows of seating. Behind us sat anyone who felt like coming for the day to support either my husband or myself. Maria, who was as encouraging and positive as ever, sat next to my two sisters. They had arrived shaken having just had an accident on the motorway ice as they drove to court but resolved and resolute to still make it to stand by my side. Their determination to put their scare aside accentuated their persistent determination to sacrifice themselves, battling with me at any cost, for the return of their nephews and niece whom they adored.

We fumbled around in disbelief at the reason we found ourselves sitting in such a formidable venue. The tension in the room could have been cut only by a chainsaw as it thickened the air and smelt of poisonous cruelty. It seemed unbelievable that the man who sat only a few seats from mine was the one who vowed to stand by my side, for richer or for poorer and in sickness and in health. If indeed I was ill, why was he not by my side protecting me from all that could possibly lie ahead and all that faced me at this time?

He sat there with his head in his hands and I felt sick to the core at the thought of the excessive grief and suffering that had been deposited on our vulnerable and undeserving children. I could barely come to terms with the role he had to play in all of this. I felt their pain lay on his shoulders and I wondered if he could be totally removed from all that they had endured. As we waited, I thought also of my in-laws and how they had so fiercely driven this whole case, aware too that alone, Jonathan would have been incapable of having them removed. I imagined their self-deception envisioning 'rescuing' their grandchildren, but all the while were ripping their little lives apart.

At that moment the doors opened and we stood as two wigged judges entered the room, one a well-known Lord whose court decisions frequented the British newspapers. He read out the case and heavily criticised Dr Harwell, which I liked. He made it very clear that he was not my treating psychiatrist and had been unethical in diagnosing me and instructed that he was not to be used again in any of the future proceedings. He questioned additionally the motives of Jonathan's family using him when very clearly there was no other information to point to Borderline Personality Disorder or to any other form of mental illness.

Evidence was given from both sides, the opposition highlighting the usual eating disorders, suicide intentions, self-harm and emotional abuse of the children. Interestingly, they had not one piece of 'hard' evidence to present, only writings from family members illustrating their distorted version of the truth and I felt a desperation arise in them as they grasped they had nothing on me.

My counsel read out the Social Services' mental health assessment which highlighted a tumultuous marriage and exhaustion from young children. A second psychiatric report was then referred to, that Victim Support had paid to have done privately at the Priory Hospital not wishing any possibility for incongruity. It said:

> *"On the basis of my interview today, I am not able to identify any evidence that Lily is suffering from any form of mental illness and certainly I have not seen any evidence that would suggest to me that she is suffering from Borderline Personality Disorder."*

The two reports voiced an identical opinion and cleared my name so plainly, it was as if the two psychiatrists had rehearsed the same speech.

A report then from the nursery articulated beautifully the close relationship between Annie and I, expressing sorrow that she had been removed so abruptly and brutally, and highlighted how damaging it would be for her at the age of three. I allowed myself to smile a little as she read out what I interpreted to be compliments regarding the bond between Annie and I, the laughter and joy between us, how I was at the nursery door twice a day and involved in all of her care. It highlighted how Annie was a happy, settled child; creative, popular, interested, focused and that she was clearly missed by the nursery team who hoped for her imminent return.

> *"We were recently inspected by OFSTED and she spoke at length to the inspector who remarked on Lily's good understanding of child development and welfare."*

The infant school report was not that dissimilar and presented positive and decisive evidence in my favour. It was followed by my GP and health visitor statements, similarly encouraging, specifying they knew the children and I well. They had no concerns, and also praised my care of all three children who they saw regularly, both in their practice and at our home.

Although my legal team disclosed evidence written by professionals that was conclusive and concrete, I could not anticipate a positive outcome as it was too dangerous to follow that train of thought in my mind. I could not dare hope for the children's return and each time I thought of their little faces, I pushed the image far away because I was vulnerably close to being disappointed again. It was easier to accept that the system I was in was corrupt and that the truth would be irrelevant, even though it was as clear as clear could be that my husband was on a mission to destroy me. I perceived that his behaviour was becoming erratic and I imagined him using any sharpened tool in his hand to bring about my fall.

We broke for lunch and returned to hear further evidence which included the judge's request to hear directly from Social Services, as to what their involvement actually was and why they had embroiled themselves, when they had clearly not carried out any statutory assessments. The opposition used the Social Service files as evidence to prove they had concerns about my relationship with the children, reading comments from Sasha Mumford and their legal representative Nareet Whan who (without ever meeting me) had written:

> *"We are seriously concerned re the mother's well-being."*
> *"The mother has mental health issues and must only have supervised contact with the children."*
> *"If the mother makes contact with the children we shall put them into care."*

In the absence of any official reports though, either initial assessments or core assessments, it was not clear to the judge nor anyone else listening to the evidence where these statements had originated from, or what Social Services were basing their evidence on. The reality was they had documented what my husband and his family had been communicating. This would all become apparent in time, but I guess the judge needed to be clear, and I was happy that he was seeking further authentication in court. He was shrewd and was not accepting any submission without verifying its origin.

Maybe at last the truth would be revealed and I felt a glimmer of hope I would witness Social Services taking the stand and their files being ripped apart and exposed. I anticipated them, at very least, being cautioned by an angry judge who would reveal their unjust and corrupt practice in communicating only what my husband and his family were saying. At best justice would truly prevail and they would be held responsible for supporting my husband in abducting the children. I wished and hoped that my mother-in-law would be admonished for abusing her influence and manipulating her knowledge of the system she had previously been involved with. We were of course in the Royal Courts of *Justice*. The truth however was not to emerge. Social Service communication came through that not only had they declined to appear, but they suddenly announced they had received an anonymous phone call. The anonymous caller left a message to say:

> *"I heard the mother communicate that if she received the children home she would murder them."*

The court came to an abrupt standstill and a piercing silence filled the air and we adjourned to the following day. My children were spending another night away from home and I was feeling pushed beyond the limits I thought I could endure, as yet more poison intoxicated the proceedings.

It had been a long day and sleep was something I had come to live without, but my body ached. I left the court with Belle, leaving Laura to collect her children from school and we paced the subways of the underground as we tried to find our way home. The internal maps in our minds however were messed up like a satellite navigation system that had lost its connection and the auto-pilot failed to kick in. We wandered around aimlessly lost, whilst the events that had taken place in court stole our attention. It was hard to read tube signs and the maps looked confusing as we discussed 'how', or 'who', or 'what on earth had just happened'.

It was looking clear that a decision could have been made to return the children, as all the evidence was in favour of my innocence. We were so close to the impossibility of any judge being able to justify their removal for any longer, yet out of the blue the tides had turned and murder had become the new threat. If I had my children returned to me I was apparently planning to kill them. It was as though madness had really sunk in, and my mind surreally went anywhere possible, searching for answers and explanations. I asked myself if I could even consider the possibility of killing my children. Had I said it? If I had, why would I be fighting for their return and what would my motive be? Maybe I was truly mad and this was just evidence that my husband was correct. I needed to be locked away and if I simply accepted it then maybe I could get some help. Was I safe? Who was I? Scared was a word that was at this moment seemed tame and the dictionary held no other choice; terror would not describe it, nor fear, nor fright, nor dread, nor horror. Panic and shock stilled me to the core and I froze into the arctic of my mind. Between us we questioned, we examined and we interviewed our memories. I had to write a statement to the court for the next day and I wrote the truth. 'I had never said I was going to kill my children'.

On the 19th of December we reconvened in the same seats, on the wooden rows resembling antiquated pews in a church, with the same faces that had been there the day before. The door was opened at the front by an assistant and I was reminded of childhood visits to the circus, when someone not that dissimilar looking would pull back a curtain and an intense air of expectancy would linger, as no one knew which animal would be brought in or which act we were to watch.

The judges entered, peering through glasses precariously sitting on the ends of their noses and glanced my way. This time however I knew the routine and I was sure of its outcome. The evidence would be heard and the children would remain in the permanent care of their father, or truthfully in the care of their grandparents, and Maya who was with them, while my husband continued to travel overseas for work. It was inevitable that justice would not come my way and I felt at the mercy of that fate, yet still inside me I simply longed to hope. I was in a place that reflected an acceptance of injustice, manipulation, lies and cruelty and I was torn between succumbing to the system that would master its own outcome and hoping that truth would prevail.

The affidavits were read first by my counsel and then the opposition, and then a statement from Social Services who mentioned the anonymous caller. It named a lady who was a mother of a child at Harry's school and it all made sense. She was close friends with Simon who was at University with Jonathan, and Simon and his wife had supported my husband in gathering evidence against me. They were a family well known in the village for involving themselves in everyone else's business and for delving into the affairs of others that they knew nothing about. Although it all added up, I was saddened by the motive in their hearts. They had children like me and I wondered how they could put them to sleep at night and carry the guilt of what they had done to mine. It was mind blowing. They had on their hands the anguish and pain that my children were suffering and they had no idea of what it meant for them to be kept away from home for any longer.

Surprisingly however, the judges seemed unfazed by all they heard and suggested the evidence was not strong enough to accuse me of the ability to murder my own children. It intimated as well that they were sceptical of a lot of evidence in the files. Jonathan had documented to say that Social Services told him to take the children, but in their notes we read:

> *"With regard to my client department 'advising' your client to remove the children from the matrimonial home, I am instructed that the Local Authority did not 'advise' your client to remove the children."*

The judges examined my statement and moved on and a ray of light shone through the court window as though someone outside purposefully drew back the blinds.

They discussed all the submissions in front of them and then presented, again heavily criticizing Judge Oppelt at Brentford County

Court who had indeed summed up to bring the children home but never did so. I celebrated the indignation shown by the examining judge, that the children were not returned home and his list of criticisms towards a judge who had acted irresponsibly and unprofessionally in my view. He emphasised the basic human rights of a child and the suffering they had all so obviously endured. He suggested that the father might bear some malice towards his wife, because he could find no evidence that the mother was a bad mother, yet he had extracted the children from her care twice without reference to the court. He mentioned that they had not only been removed from their mother, but Harry from his school, Annie from her nursery and Alfred, as a 14 month old from a mother who had never previously been separated from him overnight. He stated that they were also removed from the only home they had known and their local familiar environment.

He went on to query what arrangements had been put into place, stating that the father worked in London and was expected to travel as part of his work. He suggested that full-time care by paternal grandparents would be justified if there was evidence provided to the court that the mother was disabled, incapacitated from giving primary care, or if the mother presented any risk to the children. However, he demonstrated that it was not accepted by Judge Oppelt whose primary finding was that the mother had established by her own evidence and evidence of others that she was not so incapacitated. There was not even an indication that the children were thriving in the care arranged by the father. The testimony that two of the three children had reacted adversely was also ominous and he mentioned that these early signs if not heeded, often led to significant risks.

Then suddenly as if a clock had chimed, the world stood still and there was a malignant silence. A pause, a hesitation, a suspension of even the air particles that enabled us to breathe. The judge stood up and made the announcement that he saw no evidence justifying the abrupt removal of the children, and made orders to return them home to their mother forthwith. They were to be dropped off by their father the next morning and returned from the grandparents' care to mine. The interim residence order was decided and the ruling was made. The children would reside with me and have contact with their father every second weekend.

My wildest dream had materialised and my heart stopped suddenly, almost as though a train had hit its buffers. The difference on this occasion however was that the shock, for the first time in seemingly ages, was brought on by favourable news as opposed to bad. I was speechless, I was numb, but I turned and hugged all those who had come to support me in court today; my sisters, my friends and my amazing legal team. Tears of elation rolled down my face and pictures of my beautiful children appeared in my mind, as I imagined them soon running to leap into my arms. The joy of that moment was ineffable, but it was a tangible reality that no one could now steal. I didn't dare look at my husband to see what his reaction was, nor to the faces of his two good friends who had come to support him today. In fact I didn't consider anyone's expressions. I was in such a state of euphoria that the building could have collapsed around me and I would never have noticed. My gaze was fixed firmly on the little bodies I would soon be holding in my arms.

CHAPTER NINE

The interim residence order was returned to me and the children were to be delivered from Dorset the next day. It was the most triumphant moment in my life. Justice had finally conquered a distressing series of events and a devastating atrocity. I had my first proper night's sleep in three months and knew my children would be safe. They were to leave the unfamiliar and foreign home of grandparents and come back to their cots, beds and toys. It was only five days until Christmas but it had barely sunk in. I had no money, I was pregnant and Jonathan had kept the family car, but it was a time to celebrate and rejoice.

Suddenly I noticed the carols in the streets, and 'Hark the Herald Angels Sing' echoed so loudly that it seemed as though angels had indeed come and sung everywhere in the village where we lived. Fairies and Santa's elves which adorned shop windows for the festive season, came alive and danced with ecstasy in recognition of the victory that had prevailed. I noticed Christmas trees in bay windows of the Victorian houses which lined the streets. Shop displays suddenly advertised a party, with tinsel, wrapped gifts and expectation. More than anything the cold bitter dark days had turned to warmth and light, as I looked with comfort at the beds where the children would return to sleep each night.

Friends dropped money through the letterbox and small gifts arrived to welcome the children home. As I wondered where the food would come from, with little money in my account, I responded to a knock on the door, and the arrival of a quantity of provisions so large it was to keep us going for weeks. The local church had organised an internet supermarket delivery and we were provided with not just the basics, but chocolates, wine and surplus food for the freezer. I wondered how what I once accepted as the monotony of everyday life could instantly awaken in me such pleasure. As I received this incredible gift of food, I knew something inside me had changed for the better; I would have an inability to take anything for granted ever again.

The second knock on the door was a sound I recognized; little people and infant hands straining to hit the door knocker, whilst also struggling to keep hold of teddies in palms and toys under their arms. My children had returned and the tears rippled down my cheeks as I scooped them all up and hugged them together, never wishing to put them down or let go of the feeling of holding their little bodies so close to mine. I didn't notice the car being emptied, their possessions deposited, or the sound of the engine as Jonathan drove off in the background. I sat on the sofa wiping away a river that flowed down my cheeks and I felt a jubilation that I had never known. The stillness of the moment defined a peace in the atmosphere, which hit my exhausted body to finally anesthetize the pain I had felt for so long.

Together we sat, our bodies and arms entwined, treasuring each heart beat that measured our time together and a relief that we were reunited. The children were as happy as I had ever seen them, so excited and thrilled to be home, chatting at a hundred miles an hour and asking the questions they had kept inside for so long. They clung to me, grabbing every part of my being, holding, kissing and wrapping their little bodies around mine. Yet there was a grief present and a loss in each one of us. What had frightened us all over the past three months had anchored, surfacing in faces that were traumatised, sullen, withdrawn, fearful and lost. Tears came without the crying and things were said without words, it was like attempting to celebrate in a war zone and trying to live when we thought we had died.

Harry, who had barely existed without a hovering smile on his face in his carefree little world, stared into space with the weight of the universe on his shoulders, resonating abandonment. I worried how I would begin to unpack his feelings of loss. At five he had expressed I had died, as it was the only way his mind would justify me ever leaving the little boy I adored so much. I had been by his side as he learnt to feed, to crawl and to walk. I held his hand when he started nursery and school. I encouraged every transition as he grew and matured, from no longer being an only child but the eldest of three. I was there to put plasters on bleeding knees, to read him stories in bed at night, bath him and cuddle him, nurse him through sickness and talk him through each day, preparing him, planning and debriefing with him. Then I was gone with no explanation and he had no advance warning to prepare him.

He knew I would never have abandoned him and he perceived intuitively that I would never have left him with grandparents in what felt like a rigid and regimented home, where love as he had known was denied. I had died and he suddenly had to become a man—he had to be strong to cope with my loss. I saw immediately that he embraced a solid determination for strength and survival, and knew there was a long road ahead to build trust again in a boy so broken. He walked around the house with a pretense that nothing was wrong, but I could see there was an iron curtain that had come up around him, which was necessary to protect him from the outside world that had violated him so badly, and to also hide the devastation that lay within.

Annie, being more outwardly emotional and sensitive, was increasingly verbal, articulating clearly all her concerns. She chatted her way through the confusion, trying to understand whether she was at home to stay or to be taken yet another time. She longed to remain and pleaded for me to not leave her, as I had been forced to do on each hourly visit she had been awarded.

At three she was too young to comprehend all that had gone on and telling her that she would now be with me always was no compensation for the desperation she felt. She clung to me and I could not hold her tight enough as she squeezed me in the hopes it would bring the security she needed. She followed me around the house and watched my every move. Like an octopus she adhered to my legs and arms, pulling at my clothing, needing to be held with no physical distance between us. She was a child with a huge heart, which she wore on her sleeve and it remained visible no matter what coverings she would clothe herself with. Her eyes were the voice of her soul and pierced me with a pain and a loss that went deep, eating to the core of me. The more I hugged her, the more I felt the separation anxiety that was buried inside. I wondered how many long years it would take for her to heal and once more become the happy, bubbly, independent girl she was made to be. My beautiful little Annie hurt so badly and there was no remedy that could take her discomfort away and no plaster to cover the wounds. She was raw and suffering, and there was nothing I could do.

Alfred, just 17 months, would be picked up or put down, he would be cuddled or caressed but he continued to show no expression. It was as though he had been given a face but had no countenance. No matter what I did, he stared into a lost place that didn't exist. Of all the children he had the strongest of wills and a determination that had been admirable from birth, knowing what he wanted and what he didn't and expressing himself with such clarity that there was no messing around in one's response. At the same time he was handsomely blond and as affectionate as any child could have been made to be, adoring cuddles and contact and preferring to be held every minute of his day, not because he wasn't fiercely independent but because he was fuelled by love and captivated in returning all he was given. He was a wise man on young shoulders and it was as though he had been here before. As his mother I could see there was an evident confusion in him suggesting what had taken place over the past few months never should have been. I wished he had been able to talk and get out all that was inside; that he could scream out 'I needed you Mummy', or 'I hated you for not being there', but there was just a haunted silence and a look that was disturbing to see.

In me there was sheer exhaustion. It was the day I had not dared to imagine, because of fear that it would be denied. I was confused, as though joy had been plaited and twisted together with loss and weakness, which combined had knocked me out. I needed to build up my strength. I needed to sleep, eat, debrief and heal, as every one of the eighty long and desperate days had taken its toll. They had become knitted together like wire that was barbed, and every spike dug into my body and wrapped me brutally into my own secret prison.

Pregnancy by this time marked the four month stage and I had a long way to go carrying a growing child inside me, yet ironically I knew it was a more secure place for it to be right now than the disfigured and disoriented world outside. With the baby, there was a total of five of us with not dissimilar needs and yet what those were I could barely discern. What I did acknowledge, however, was that I was alone. Instead of having a husband by my side to hold me in his arms and reassure me, the hope of family life with him around was currently a long distant dream. My marriage had ended and I felt a weight of responsibility like I had never known before. I was worryingly burdened by financial hardship, emotional trauma, social stigma, fear of the future and physical fatigue.

If I thought I was to sleep that first night of the children's return I was mistaken. I fed and bathed Harry, Annie and Alfred and read them stories as they lay in my arms smelling sweetly of the shampoo we always used. Their neatly folded pyjamas sat there glaringly as they had awaited their return for so long, amongst the piles of tiny clothes neglected but freshly folded. The giggles came and went as we read the stories they brought off the shelves and thrust into my hands. Eager to be reminded of the caterpillar so hungry, we read of how he ate the holes through their book and how the rabbit told them how much he loved his mummy. We read *The Whale and the Snail* and talked about the giraffe who couldn't dance and we made up our own stories with happy endings, paradoxically drawing us further into the precarious place we were presently in. We had been gifted a happy ending but I wondered if there could be such a thing.

The house felt a warm and safe place to be, and although the wind howled outside there was a presence of peace inside. The harmony of reconciliation induced a sleep in us as we remained adhered to one another in my big huge bed in our home. It was a sleep however that was not secure.

Only an hour had passed before the first nightmare began. Harry screamed for his mummy and Annie sat upright, frightened as tears rolled down her cheeks. Alfred followed closely behind and contributed to the discord as if repeating a pattern of previous nights. With the reassurance of a whisper or the touch of my hand one by one they would sleep and wake, and sleep and wake and although deprived of months of rest myself, I lay enchanted in joy, remaining awake if only to watch them and smile at the gift of their return.

CHAPTER TEN

Christmas came and went and communicated the birthing of something new. The presents around the imaginary tree that we could not afford were donated by a charity known to Maria, who gave to children who would otherwise go without. As though abundance had arrived, we were each given a generous gift we could all unwrap. Unable to travel without the car, we were taken in by a local family of nine who knew of our plight. We ate the most welcome Christmas dinner I had ever had, served by friends who cooked a true festive feast. Together we toasted to celebrate the gift of my children's return and to all that would lie ahead.

It would be a future that would deviate from the plans I had made and certainly would be different from what I had expected. I no longer worried what time my husband would be home or whether I wore the right clothes for the day. It mattered little what the shops were selling or who was having the dinner party that week. My concentration switched to focussing on a smile, a word, a leaf, a drop of rain and I noticed every small detail of what made our days tick. Life in itself had become a gift and each day brought the realisation of how lucky I was to have my children with me, knowing it was something I would never again ever take for granted. At the same time it was hard because we were no longer a 'family' as we had known it. The children's father had gone, friends who were suspicious stayed away, there was no financial provision and I was expecting another baby. Added to that my life was still dominated by solicitor's letters, sent at an alarming rate by a man who would not settle for having lost the most recent court hearing.

In January, Harry returned to his infant school at the end of the road with a little trepidation to the class he had left. He was nervous as to the welcome he would receive as his greatest joy was the anticipation of seeing his best friend again whom he had grown up with during the past four years.

Billy and he had both been the only children in their respective families welcoming together the arrival of their two sisters at the same time when they were both aged two. Their shared displacement as 'only children' brought a bond that would see them stick together as the girls grew and began to make their presence known. They were both obsessed with train tracks and would play for hours at each other's houses, being entertained by the various engines or trucks they had collected, and influenced by the adventures in the train books they were reading. They went to the same mother and toddler playgroups and then started Montessori nursery school together, where they would always be seen sitting, singing or playing together, often to the exclusion of other children.

Returning to the infant school however brought one of the hardest lessons Harry had to learn, whilst in such a fragile and vulnerable condition. At the tender age of five, his best friend's mother no longer wanted Billy to play with Harry. She blanked me at the school gates and I was utterly heartbroken to realise that the great friendship we had shared during such an important part of my life had ended. Harry was devastated. He was so little and had no resources to deal with another loss in his life and he withdrew even further into his own little world needing to protect himself from all that seemed so cruel. Billy's mother never explained why she had cut off the friendship and at no time expressed her view as to all that had gone on, but simply walked out of our lives and then daily walked past us as if we never existed.

She was not alone. Many other mothers, whom I had known well, turned the other way when they saw me walk down the street. Some crossed the road to avoid their own obvious embarrassment of not knowing how they would deal with me if I said hello. Others simply walked straight past as if they had never seen me before, let alone shared a chapter of their lives with me. I heard rumours that Jonathan had been talking to them and one mother confessed, he had told her very charmingly that he was taking the children away to protect them from me, because I was mentally ill and abusing them. He was a charismatic man and they had all fallen for his tales of how much he loved me and how sad he was, but he was doing this 'for the best' and requested their support saying, "if you assist her she will not get the help she needs."

These people who walked away had spent many days a week at my house over the past four years and knew me intimately. Not only that, but they had watched me day after day bringing up my children, playing with them, laughing with them and caring for them while all of our husbands worked long hours and travelled overseas. I had been a good friend to them and had been invited to their houses; we had walked in the park and shared in the looking after of each others' children. We took turns during sickness, for doctor's visits, or unavoidable clashes in timetables, where we had to be in two places at once and they had trusted me with their own children for periods of care. I was unsure how they could know me so well and yet currently shut me out of their lives because my husband—with whom they had barely been acquainted—convinced them I must be harming my children. I could not believe they had not been by my side and I longed to understand all they thought and talked of, but knew intuitively it was not my place to ask.

By quite remarkable contrast, other class mums stepped out of their comfort zone and there was nothing more they could have done for me when they heard what had happened. One couple who had a daughter in Harry's class invited me over regularly when I had been without the children and generously shared meals, without even realising I had no food at home to feed myself. They researched child abduction on the internet putting me in contact with various charities, made phone calls and even organised a private audience with our local Member of Parliament, to petition on my behalf for the return of the children. They kindly also welcomed the children home with such great pleasure and they became very precious to us, adopting us all back into a tangible human love whilst holding us emotionally for a long time during the bleak seasons we yet had to face. They were an extraordinary family who opened their hearts to receive us at this lonely time.

At the same stage that Harry returned to school, Annie started at the little infant nursery attached to the property. She loved being near her big brother, seeing him each day as we walked in at noon through the courtyard where he played. Being a sociable child she loved having close friends and was always popular, being quick to make new acquaintances. Although she was obviously lacking in confidence at this time in her life, I was appreciative that my own friends nurtured her relationship with their children, knowing the importance of her feeling loved during this momentous period.

While the other two were at school, Alfred and I walked in the park and sat by the river, enjoying a couple of hours each day to spend together. I saw it as a crucial time to rebuild trust and restore the bond that had previously been so strong between us. We would throw balls across the grass to each other, watch the butterflies flutter and chase the birds around the lawn and he would laugh as some joy began to return. These were very special times and genuinely much needed for a little boy who had always had such an interest in life and all that went on around him. During these bonding afternoons he never missed a chance to point at something he had seen, or communicate enthusiasm in what he did.

Our lives developed a routine that was important in stabilising us all. At weekends we would visit our allotment, where the children had been used to spending time digging for worms, planting seeds or bulbs and turning over the compost heap. They particularly loved having winter bonfires to burn dried wood from the previous year's harvest, and they would also squeal in satisfaction as they toasted their marshmallows on sticks when the flames had died back. It was of great satisfaction to return to the outdoors and its healing cycles of life.

Our friends welcomed the children home and life was lived day by day as we tried to resurrect and rebuild, like the reassembling of a huge Lego tower that had been destroyed. Some days were good and others were hard; as the true level of confusion the children had suffered revealed how deeply disturbed they were. I had requested counselling for them all to help them verbalise and express their anxieties and fears, but Jonathan had put a stop to it in court leaving them to suffer the effects of their pain.

CHAPTER ELEVEN

In awarding the interim residence order to me, Lord Thornton at the Court of Appeal ruled that the whole family should be seen by the Cassel Hospital in Ham. He ordered that we be assessed by Dr Kimberly, insisting that the report should be sent to both solicitors upon completion. He also stressed that there should be no doubt at all that this was not a referral to assess the mother in isolation. However, alarm bells rang in my mind, as this was the original recommendation of Dr Harwell, and Lord Thornton had been wise enough to dismiss him off the case. Although the judge was insistent that this would be an assessment of not just me but the dynamics of the whole family, including Jonathan, trepidation and apprehension perforated my intuition. I discerned a foreknowledge that I was entering into another 'set up'; evidence of which had clearly displayed in one of the emails from my father-in-law, dated 6 months previously. Jonathan was corresponding with Dr Harwell, who in writing recommended I be referred to the Cassel, where Dr Kimberly was a lead specialist in BPD.

The Cassel, founded in 1919 was used originally for the treatment of 'shell shock' victims. It had over time developed behavioural rather than medicinal techniques of group and individual psychotherapy, and was pioneered into a therapeutic community in the 1940s. It was today well known for providing specialist assessment and treatment services for families with intractable personality problems, where all other avenues of help from mental health, children's and social care services had been exhausted.

In theory it would seem the ideal solution to expose some of the suffering that we had all endured during the past few months, both in the hands of my in-law family and also with some of the professionals. In my opinion however, any referral to an institution that had been recommended by Dr Harwell, was only opening a door to a dangerous opportunity for further mishandling of my children. The Court of Appeal had made it very clear that Dr Harwell was not a jointly instructed expert, and indeed raised concerns about offering a diagnosis of someone who was not his patient. I wondered whether he would be well known to both Dr Kimberly and the Cassel.

This was not the only reason for wanting to steer clear of this institution. The last thing Harry, Annie and Alfred needed right now was further intrusion into their lives. What they required was therapy to enable them to deal with their own fragile situation, not an investigation into family dynamics for the benefit of court. They wanted some healing time in a familiar environment, or one at least where the criteria was individually focussed. Certainly an institution seeking to extract information from their internal world, which was so vulnerable, was an invasion of their privacy at such a crucial time. In all honesty, many of the 'experts' I had met during the last few months, had cared so little for the lives they involved themselves with and the last thing I wanted to do was engage again with professionals whose priority seemed first to protect their reputations, then their positions and their jobs.

The children and I needed to re-group, resettle, be left alone to lick our wounds and cuddle up on sofas doing puzzles together and telling stories. We needed to bake together, talk together, laugh together and play together and be surrounded by people and things that were familiar, secure and nurturing. If we needed anything less at this time, it was to be thrust into the world of psychologists, psychiatrists, therapists, psychoanalysts, and psychotherapists. During the events of the past several months I had lost all confidence in organisations and institutions and my intuition perceptively warned me to steer clear of what I smelt as 'danger'.

We scarcely had six weeks at home when I received in the post via my solicitor an itinerary of dates that we were to attend the Cassel. We had barely worked out which side of the day was up and which was down before we were ordered to appear yet again in front of strangers. In various combinations I was to be assessed with the children and without them. I was also to be seen alone and it was the same with Jonathan over a number of days spanning a ten week period. I held the interim residence order, but this was dependent on further reports which would enable the courts to decide where the children would permanently reside. I was aware we were all sitting in a time capsule that could explode at any minute.

For our first assessment the children and I had to attend the Cassel together. It was against my wishes and the last thing on earth I wanted to do but I prepared the children. I told them we would be meeting lovely kind people who would help us all and we could play with their toys and have a pleasant time while they talked about how we could be helped. The reality could not have been further from all I had discussed. The children and I walked into a room with a lady who sat officially upright on her wooden chair, legs crossed and arms folded. She pointed her head towards the ceiling and held her neck high as she pouted and introduced herself as a child psychologist, "I am Beatte Schmidt. Has your mother explained why you are here? Do you know who we are?" There was a stunned eerie silence and the children moved closer to grab me, nervous arms wrapping around my body and legs. It seemed impossible to me that this lady could have appeared more severe if she had tried, and I was reminded of other personality types I had previously met in Social Services, who should never have been allowed to have contact with children, let alone earn a living from doing so.

The male adult psychologist also in the room presented as no different and I wrongly assumed he was Dr Kimberly who had been appointed by the court. He completed the same ceremonious introduction as if the training had taken place in some Russian army. Silence descended in the room. I said nothing, as no words could emerge from my mouth and I felt the prickling of my instinct telling me we were entering into something that was not safe.

There was no warmth or no peace and nothing in that room convinced me or the children that these people were genuinely interested in our well-being. When we were then moved into another room, the children were told to play with toys as if they were beings that somehow could perform on demand. They had to move from the safety of their mother's side and all that represented, to play with toys that they had no interest in, as though on a stage being watched by a crowd. The children were obviously feeling threatened and uneasy and rightly so. To reassure them I sat on the floor with them, choosing to opt out of the chair positioned in the corner and manoeuvre myself uncomfortably, now seven months pregnant, on the hard wood floor encouraging the children to explore the toys.

Alfred clung to me and was having none of the insistence that he leave my side. I managed to gently encourage Annie to investigate the dolls' house which she was usually inclined towards. Harry cautiously dragged the building blocks nearer me, keeping one eye firmly fixed on where I was and sat then on my lap as he began to build. I continued to engage them in their play as we were all formally interviewed about our lives; who played with who, how we managed day to day living and whether we were coping. The atmosphere remained cold and the nervousness in the room was tangible but I stayed focused on encouraging the children. I smiled at the correct promptings and cautiously answered loaded questions.

It was an awkward two hours and I experienced huge relief to walk from the room and remove my children from the oppressive confines of the environment that day, but I also felt uneasy as I drove us all back home in our hire car. Intuitively I knew that all was not well, but at the same time could not put my finger on the apprehension I felt. I was perplexed and perturbed. I felt as though someone else other than these two people had already written a report on the children and my ability to care for them, and they were simply going through the motions of having to meet with us. Perhaps I should have listened to my instincts at the time, because later the report was to become highly contested, but I still had nine more stressful weeks to worry about the outcome.

The second visit to the Cassel was slightly different. I had been asked to bring food that I could cook in the kitchen with the children present, and I prepared well in advance for the occasion. I knew from a friend who had worked at the Cassel that there was a one-way viewing wall, where I would be watched and monitored, and having felt so uneasy previously had wanted no room for mis-judgement this time.

I took vegetables which I sliced and cookie cutters for the children to stamp out shapes which they loved doing at home. They wore their little aprons which we had made and rolled up their sleeves, rehearsing routines they loved, as they cut out cucumber dinosaurs and the equivalent of gingerbread men but in vegetable form. Harry, Annie and Alfred were happy sitting up on the stools at the kitchen units and turned to the cookie mixture I had been making alongside, once they had finished the vegetables.

The boiled eggs had cooled from the saucepan and I gave the children some colour pens which they used to draw faces on their eggs, so we could eat a 'jungle lunch'. I moved the children to a table nearby which was clear from flour and food peelings, and settled them to some colouring, while I wiped away the mess and washed all we had used. I laid the table finding the plates and small knives and forks, put out the napkins from our bag and filled their little cups with water.

There was pleasant happy buzz as the children hummed and showed me their colourings while I encouraged them, to keep them focused. It was the third appointment they had attended at the Cassel, as they had also visited with their father and so seemed more relaxed, as familiarity was being established. We were left alone in the kitchen with a supervisor, who seemed kind and I guessed quickly her role was purely to assist if needed. I remained aware that there were recordings being made behind the mirrored wall, and presumed they were making notes on relationships, dynamics, and behaviour. I imagined they were interested in how I coped with a normal daily routine having been given a precursory set of instructions.

I was pleased that there was no conflict with the children, but then there rarely was, unless they were tired, hungry or sick. The room seemed peaceful as we all ate together and Annie and Harry laughed with enchantment at the shapes that had slightly distorted through the cooking process. We had not been told there was a time limit and so excited squeals came when I produced three icing syringes and added colours to the icing sugar. Shrieks of amusement were released as fast as the icing from the tubes, adding a messy decoration to the biscuits, which were then rapidly eaten. The children were safe and happy and everything had gone as well as I could have hoped. We were free to leave.

My third visit was traumatic and upset me deeply. It was an arranged meeting between Jonathan and I, and the two psychologists whom I had met with the children only a few weeks ago. It was a day that particularly frightened me, as I felt unsafe around my husband and extremely vulnerable so late on in my pregnancy. Jonathan was interviewed and they clearly related well to him, possibly responding to his charm and what I felt was a sophisticated ability to misrepresent the truth. Smiles passed from them to him and agreeing nods as he spoke and I felt awkward as I picked up on the non verbal communication between them all. Clearly he was a wonderful father and an adoring husband who could not do enough for his wife. It was a tragedy that she was mentally sick, but he hoped that they would support his view that she needed hospital admission, or sadly, sectioning. Then all would be well, as he could then be with her again because he loved so much. Again grins of sympathy passed over their faces, like clouds revealing a change in the weather and they glanced from my husband to me with acknowledging looks. Their body language appeared to align with what I was noticing and I sensed it revealed that they had already made assumptions about me, as though fitting me into a stereotype which ticked all the boxes on their lists.

I could see many writings about me in the Social Services files so clearly in the back of my mind as they spoke, that the papers may as well have been on my lap, as the adults moved positions in their chairs to tell me it was my turn to be interviewed. I wondered what I could say as their questions seemed loaded and I felt incredibly exposed sitting there with only eight weeks to go until I delivered my next baby. Somehow I understood I needed so much more than could be offered in that room on that day. I felt silenced by the looks on their faces as they glanced at me with almost accusation in their eyes, that I could be causing this man such much worry in his life. I left in tears and felt so very alone as I drove home, again facing the fear of all that he was capable of doing.

CHAPTER TWELVE

Isolation gripped me deeply as I looked out of the windscreen of the car and saw what seemed normal lives around. Couples walked together hand in hand, men mowed lawns, women pushed push-chairs, children walked dogs, builders climbed ladders, cyclists rode by and I wondered whether I would ever be able to enjoy life again without the constant worry of all that lay ahead. I felt I lived in a hidden and mysterious world that no one knew anything of.

Maria had been right that I should choose very carefully who I confided in and she was wise in her words. There is a phrase, 'there is no smoke without fire' and it was interesting how I interpreted it on so many faces of people I knew. I had always been good at reading minds with accuracy and frequently saw 'guilt' written in large letters in the subconscious of many of the people around. They were like large characters of the alphabet scribed—almost similar to the Hollywood sign, seen set into the hilltop of the Santa Monica Mountains in Los Angeles—which my imagination could see from afar. I longed to shout out my innocence but could not do so and something in me knew it was not the right thing to undertake. The depths of the deceit, corruption, injustice and misrepresentation that had gone on were painfully exhausting to reveal, and so I kept my mouth shut and just lived each day as it came.

I had a dear friend Jemma who spent much time looking after the children when I had to attend the Cassel, appear in court, or visit my solicitor in London. I remembered how she had counselled me well when I had to reappear at the school gates, after the children had returned home. I had heard much of the gossip spreading around the village we were in and I had asked her how I could show my face when so many mums had judged me, forming their own opinions in the absence of me ever revealing all that had gone on. Jemma gave shrewd advice and told me to hold my head up high, as I had done nothing wrong. She encouraged me to walk into school with my beautiful children allowing mums to watch as I did so. They were gentle and yet fundamental words of wisdom, which were a tremendous support to me at the time and I honoured her friendship tremendously.

In the absence of me wishing to speak the truth, no one locally knew of the problems I faced in my marriage, which were typical in a relationship with a spouse dependent on alcohol. These were self-absorption, inability to see reality, denial, irresponsibility, poor communication, lack of intimacy, failure to meet obligations and an inability to follow through with promises and commitments; all of which had a profound impact on our lives. Unless one has lived with the effects of alcohol overuse, one would not understand the increased stress, embarrassment, emotional pain, anxiety, loss of intimacy and connection, helplessness and sadness that a non-alcoholic partner would face. On top of that no one knew how

Maya had become the third person in our marriage, nor were they aware of the relentless pursuit from my in-laws to have my children taken from me.

I wish I could have shouted from the rooftops that there was indeed much smoke without fire, as anyone who had been involved with Social Services or the family courts would well know. But worse than the ignorance that lay around the professional services, was the fact that most people were still unaware that the family courts were 'sworn to secrecy'. This meant that nothing that took place within its walls could be spoken about, least of all released to the press, leaving the public naive about the statistics of children removed, taken into foster care and worse still pushed through into forced adoptions. The English judicial system had managed to keep all that had happened in the family courts so far hidden from the public eye. The result of this was an obscuring of the extent of the abuse that had gone on in their hands, keeping the general public in complete ignorance of the atrocities that occurred.

I thought of the security and stability I experienced as a child in the extended family we had around and how it contrasted so enormously to what I felt right now in the hidden world I was in, and my dear mother came to my mind. Tears erupted with emotion as memories of her became as real as a film being played on a cinema screen right in front of my eyes. I saw her beautiful face and her smile which would melt any child to run into her warm, enfolding arms, yet she had sadly died before her seven grandchildren were born.

She married late and experienced an exciting life as a single lady during her 20's and 30's. She had left an all-girls convent to study at the London School of Economics and pursued a varied and eclectic career before meeting my father at her own twin's wedding and settling to raise a family she adored. As the film settings changed, I saw in my imagination my three children sitting on her lap, and such pleasure in her eyes as she recited the same stories she read to me. Behind, laid on the table on the lawn, were afternoon tea with freshly made cream cakes and small finger sandwiches filled with jam. Toys were scattered under the apple tree on a rug in the shade and her secateurs sat beside, showing where she had just pruned her roses. Emotion welled up in me like a watering can being filled and I sensed such loss that she was not around today and wondered how different things would have been if she were.

She adored young children and always spoke of her longing to watch the future generation grow, but became ill with cancer in my teens and left the world before her desire was fulfilled. My dreams at this moment were shattered sadly, as I imagined leaving this stark and alien world of a mental health institution with her by my side, or driving to collect my children from her home where the kettle would have been on. Significant as well was my sorrow for Harry, Annie and Alfred not knowing their grandmother whom they would have treasured, as much they did their grandfather. She had kept for her grandchildren the old dolls' prams, along with the babies that went inside. She had packed away the clothes she had sewn, the children's tea party sets, the double sided chalk boards and wooden brick blocks, which indicated how she had prepared ahead for their arrival. I pondered sadly and thought what her absence meant in all of our lives.

I drifted back to gritty reality as the car arrived finally at number three Kings Road and I felt pleased that the Cassel assessments had come to an end. The weeks passed by and time moved on and the children began to heal, slowly emerging from their ordeal. They began to trust with renewed faith that their home was theirs and their friends would remain part of their daily lives, but weekends continued to trouble them. The court had awarded access to Jonathan every other weekend and the children certainly needed to remain in contact with their father. Friday nights however disturbed the children because they would be taken against their wishes to all they had known to be so unsafe and they clung to me pleading not to go. They cried as they were strapped into the car, by an often agitated man who had become irritated by the new regime. His body language reflected deep anger at the loss of control over my life, which he could see was evidently becoming more settled. He was impatient as he put the children in their chairs, forcing their seat belts on and always as they drove away I hated seeing their distress. Their visits to Dorset were predictably and consistently followed by the arrival of solicitors' letters on a following Tuesday morning. By this time my mother-in-law had gathered sufficient time to document more written evidence, having just spent more time observing her grandchildren.

Harry, Annie and Alfred hopelessly despised spending two days each fortnight with them, and returning to their house only triggered post-traumatic stress from wounds that were still quite raw. This manifested as withdrawn, rude and angry behaviour in their presence and rightfully so, as they were returning to an environment that had already ripped their lives apart. Their disruptive conduct was however, to my in-laws, supporting evidence that whilst staying with me during the weekdays, I continued to abuse the children. Alarmingly they even accused me of starving them; withholding both food and water. To an outsider their writings read as so extreme that they seemed ridiculous and ludicrous. They possibly suggested they were clutching at straws. However their words affected me deeply and I wondered whether this was a worrying exposure, revealing the level of deception they held onto. If not, then it was an indication of the lengths this family would yet go, to try and break or rupture my resolve.

My husband was behaving like a stranger and could not reply to my 'hello' at the front door nor could he make eye contact, let alone acknowledge the size of my bump which was due in a few weeks' time. He had been furious that I had announced another pregnancy, and still at this late stage had not made any mention of the baby that now kicked reassuringly inside. Since his mother had claimed the pregnancy was 'impossible', she clearly hoped to prove I was unhinged or delusional. Consequently at the family's request, I had to produce medical evidence, signed by my GP and produce it to a surprised judge in court! Confirmation aside and the truth currently being clearly visible, it did little to warm Jonathan to the arrival of a fourth child and I carried his baby alone, with no acknowledgement from him of how hard that might have been.

By this stage I was extremely tired and needed to sleep during the day, which for obvious reasons was not a possibility. I was uncomfortable at night and currently lack of sleep was caused not only by the late stage of the pregnancy but by the children's restlessness too. When I did fall asleep, I was soon woken by one of them, roused by the nightmares that continued to plague them. Annie would stir often with separation anxiety and cling to me tightly, while Alfred would just need to be cuddled through the night for reassurance that I was still there. I had no one to take the children off my hands during the day so I could rest. I had no one to help with the chores, no one to pick all the toys off the floor when I could no longer reach the ground, no one to do the endless piles of washing that sat in the wicker basket. I had no one to allow me head space to even begin to work out how I would cope when the baby did arrive, and I simply longed for time to heal.

This child I was carrying was Jonathan's. It was a sibling for his three other children and another grandchild for his parents, yet somehow the subject remained off limits during any conversation we had. I began to realise through his lack of concern for me that he didn't even care about the baby and I began to see another side of my husband that had never been shown before. He appeared callous and calculating and his mission to set out to break me and destroy our lives took precedence over protecting the mother of his unborn child. In the coming weeks I would see evidence of behaviour that I never imagined he could be capable of. Yet I remained oblivious, still believing I had been through the worst.

CHAPTER THIRTEEN

June had arrived and I had six days to go until my baby was due to be born. The schools had routinely broken for their end of May half term holiday and the weather had warmed into early summer days. I wanted to enjoy the time with the children as much as possible and made plans for each day during this short break, ensuring I could maximise the time I had with Harry, Annie and Alfred before another little one would make demands on my time. We had day trips out to the local parks on buses, and borrowed a car a visit to the beach so we could enjoy a seaside day watching the fairground rides. We ate our picnic on the lawn and played on the shingle that so readily depicts the coastline in the south of England, with its traditional wooden breakwaters and smell of seaweed lining the shores.

I felt brave as I drove alone the four hour round trip from London, with three children aged five, three and one. With another one about to be born, I was so irritatingly large that my bump barely fitted under the steering wheel of the car. I wanted us to laugh and heal and I knew we needed adventures together, so we could regroup and bond before another little one entered our world.

These were very special days and the children were the happiest they had been since they had returned from their removal five months earlier, showing signs that they were beginning to overcome the trauma that had occurred. We spent precious time enjoying access to some of the most beautiful places on the outskirts of London, including Hampton Court Palace and Ham House. I witnessed new inner freedom and confidence emerge as they ran through the parks, played with friends, walked by the river, fed the ducks and wandered around in the gardens of Kew. Alongside this there was a sadness lingering, as I felt the early signs of labour on its way, because I seemed to notice wherever I went husbands held their pregnant wives' arms whilst carrying other children on their shoulders. The loneliness of my struggle to keep going was heightened by happy families playing in the park, while I lifted and carried three quite heavy children. I struggled additionally with the shopping and no car, and with months of broken sleep. It would be at this time a husband could step in and help at nights and perform tasks that intuitively a father would do, but he was not around. With so many demands on my time where I would otherwise be resting before this baby's birth, I felt plagued by exhaustion.

On my due date we had the most magical of all our cherished days. The children were singing, laughing and playing so happily in and amongst my struggle with fatigue. I counted my blessings feeling so richly fortunate, happy and grateful for the gift of these little people and the relationship we shared. The healing that was happening was a joy to see unfold and it united us in a bond of such tremendous love. There were no more scary knocks on the door. There was no more apprehension, and no more uncertainty about what lay ahead in each day. Social Services had not called or visited us once since the children had returned, showing how little they had really been concerned. It was lovely to have some space and feel a sense of freedom from the investigations that had previously beset our lives.

Although we were alone without their father, there was a peace that had emerged. With the turmoil and confusion gone, the house became warm with a tranquil sense of joy. Although the days were hard, they were also so much easier than when the children had first returned less than four months ago.

In the early evening sun we returned to the house, smelling of the scent of summer. While a friend bathed the children, I stood at our front gate chatting with a neighbour who lived over the road and discussed the impending arrival of a little baby who was currently a day late. The contrast between this peace and the brutality of what unfolded in the next moments could not have been more inordinate, nor could they have represented a greater dichotomy of extremes.

While we stood at the gate, a police car drew up in the street and I commented that I wondered to which house it was to go. As soon as I had spoken a second car drove up and parked and as it did I saw the police walk to my house and approach the gate. I had still not imagined that they were there to visit me, assuming only they just wanted to ask their way, but people in plain clothes suddenly appeared from the other car and hastily now asked me where my children were. It was like a scene from the police show 'Z Cars' that we had watched as children, or 'Softly Softly', where one's adrenaline rushed as the police exercise unfolded. Suspiciously however, the drama was at my house, at number three Kings Rd, in a happy little village where this kind of occurrence was not usually seen.

The police took my keys out of my hand which I had not yet put down and told me that they would be keeping hold of them as they entered the house. A lady, who I later discovered was from Social

Services, handed me a piece of paper stating that they had come to take the children from me. She demanded I pack their things and hand them over; telling me there was little time. The moment stood still and I was frozen to the spot.

Things were said and I heard nothing. Papers were handed for me to read but they were a blur and I could not anticipate what to do. I could not speak and could only think of my children who were now in towels coming out of the bath with my friend, whose face reflected the panic I felt. Another horror story was being played out and I didn't want my children to see or hear anything that would affect the future safety and security of our own home. My mind was a blank as time emptied itself into a black hole of eternity and I heard—like a fast-forwarded music tape—a tunnel of various sounds echoing through my head.

I paced the entranceway looking for my phone. I glanced to the right and then to the left. I then repeated the same movements, not focusing on where it had actually been placed but instinct led me in my blindness to where it lay. I somehow found the numbers on my phone which were the private contact details for my lawyer Emily Hewlett and dialled. All I could say was, "They are taking my children away. They are taking my children away." Emily—as shocked as I was—asked me to hand the phone to anyone with whom she could speak. I assumed it was so she could find out what was going on, but I couldn't even think enough to know. I passed the phone, giving it to someone who looked like an outline, or a shadow, or ghost, because my eyes couldn't even see, and I went to be with my children.

I climbed to the top of the stairs, quite an arduous task for my body that was ready to give birth. I went to where Harry, Annie and Alfred were all peering through the bannisters, watching with trepidation and fear, as though knowing something serious was going on. I took them in my arms and cuddled them, not knowing if I would ever do so again. There flowed immediately between us all, a wealth of emotion, like an electrical current that had escaped its circuit. As little as the children were, we all knew what this meant and I faced helplessly one of the most frightening moments of my life, watched by police officers in uniform at the bottom of the staircase.

As though plugged into a backup generator, I suddenly switched onto autopilot, knowing I had to go through the motions and do what I was told to do. If I was to fight what was to happen? I couldn't create a scene in front of the children and make the atmosphere more daunting for them than it was right now. I had to find some inner resolve that I knew I had not yet found, some deep courage to remain calm and make everything appear as normal and as acceptable for them as I could. It went against all human instinct, but innately I knew there was no other way. I went to get suitcases as Social Services were aggravating the atmosphere by rushing me and telling me to hurry up. I refused to be hustled by the pressure they were discharging into the atmosphere, as I felt that whatever time restriction they were under was not my issue and I wasn't going to put their needs before my children's.

On my knees, I gently dressed the children in clean pyjamas, which was a difficult exercise as my bump was annoyingly huge for me to be able to easily bend low. I could feel pain sharp inside as though the baby also felt the exasperation of what was going on in its exterior world. I had to answer all the children's questions as to who was in the house and what was going on, as I folded neatly into suitcases all that they would need if they were going to be whisked away. I talked sweetly and gently to them, desperately trying to hide my fear and spoke slowly so as to hide the panic and hostility of all that was unravelling in front of our eyes.

My phone was handed back to me by what appeared a sweet, young police lady; the look in her eye told me she knew she was not meant to be in the house that day. In her I felt an awkwardness as well as a wealth of emotion which she did not show. Emily mentioned court orders but knew not what they were about, other than the knowledge that the papers previously handed to me being the direction for the immediate removal of all three children.

I called more friends who arrived at the house in minutes. Katie and Susy, two sisters who lived not far away, who had already supported me through so much, arrived almost immediately. Not long after followed Maria, and Laura a little later, as the full abomination of all that was taking place continued to unfold. There was a silence in the house and a violent frenzy too and I moved from one room to the other as eyes watched my every move. Friends stood as statues and the children looked confused. Again I was ordered to hurry up and pack their things but I could not move quickly, as I was all over the place not knowing which way to turn.

I flitted from cuddling the children and moving from suitcases to drawers, to trying to read the papers thrust in front of my eyes, but it was as though I had never learned to read. I saw no words I could recognise on the papers with jumbled print. I saw people not faces around me and I witnessed fear like black ink, written all over the walls of my white home invaded by such an air of horror. I even heard the brutality like machine guns going off all around. I was as numb as a robot and I knew I should not, could not react, as my children required protecting. Essentially they needed to not know of all that was going on in their home, their rooms, their place of refuge.

I was aware intuitively the baby that I carried needed protecting. Something in my body was not going the way it should. My bump was hard and again a pain rushed through me, a sharp agonizing cramp that was not labour. It presented as a terrifying existence of a physical manifestation that I had not experienced before in any of my other three pregnancies. Thoughts rushed through my mind that I could possibly be losing this child who was so near to entering the world and I didn't know where to turn.

I had to protect all four of my children, unborn or not. In my desire to stay calm I anaesthetised myself in my mind and body. I sensed a wave of hypnosis drift over me and I somehow found a source of an imaginary morphine-like chemical, which rushed through my veins to temporarily sedate and transition me into an imperturbable mode of existence. It came from a primal, inbuilt instinct deep with my being, like an animal protecting its young from a predator. I shut out the world as the adrenalin rushed around my body, silencing me from the demands of the hurrying, cruel voice of the social worker looking agitatedly at the watch on her arm.

I gathered the children and sat them all on what was left of my lap. I somehow squeezed them all around my large agonizing bump. I talked of how they were going on an adventure and that I needed them to fetch their teddy bears and pack them in their little cases, ready for all that lay ahead. I could have done it myself but knew they needed to have some sense of control over what was going on, and they duly collected the animals they loved and clung to them tightly, gripping as if they knew like me this was the end. I told them that I loved them and was so proud of them and that I would see them soon, but as calm as I remained they knew that all was not right. It was a penetrating moment where I wasn't sure I would ever see my children again and pain like lightening forked through my body.

Their faces reflected the same disturbed fear I had seen so many times before on the hourly contact visits when we had been separated against our wishes. Nothing I said would convince the children that all would be well. The officers now frustrated at the time delay, manhandled them out of the house and into the marked police vehicle with their identifying blue lights still flashing.

This injustice and cruelty could never be described as they were all hurried into the police car. Harry had a desperate look and never took his eyes off me, as he put his arm around Annie, trying to protect her from what he knew was not right and climbed into the car. I carried Alfred out, still only a one year old, and refused to answer to the continued hurrying demands of Social Services. They were forcefully trying to hasten me, but in their insistence of urgency, all I felt was the weight of what these small children had endured in their short little lives.

I could see an uneasiness in the eyes of the police and wondered how they could remove children from a scene where soft music was playing, children were splashing in the bath and laughter and joy sung out of the windows into the street below. They had not been met by a mother who was screaming, nor was she shouting, nor was she drunk or on drugs, but gently calming her children.

Did these women from the police and Social Services standing in my home have their own children? Could they have ever given birth or loved the way I did? Did they know or remember what it felt like to be on their due delivery date and need the love and gentleness of at least one person around them? Did they remember what it was like to be a child and need their mother? Could they know of the pain my children would suffer right now? I assumed from what I was sensing they only understood family violence which they witnessed in the lives of some of those they dealt with. Wretchedly, they were bringing this violence into the lives of my children, and our home felt invaded by a terror we had not known before.

My mind was all over the place as I carried little Alfred to the police car door. He was crying and clinging to me, his nails digging in, and fierce were his movements as he tried to turn me back. I said nothing to Social Services and had not uttered a word to the police until I noticed that the car contained no child seats. They wanted to place my three tiny children in their vehicle and drive them away with no safety measures in place. I could contain my silence no more and spoke my first words to these supposed professionals, insisting that I would not let my children be driven away without car seats. I mentioned the law which I saw scared them, as concern set in all over their faces and they were at a standstill to know what to do.

"We are not driving them far," was the response, but I didn't care. If I had papers thrust in front of me telling me I had to hand my children over because the law said so, it was one thing, but I was not having them put in a car with no safety seats for them to be secured in.

The police had told me they were taking the children to Dorset, but shamefully and to their embarrassment, they had to tell me the truth. Jonathan was around the corner and waiting to take the children in his car. They were driving the children only a street away.

I asked them to bring my husband to the house, insisting that if they leave, it was better that they go with their father in his car than in a police car being driven away from their mother. My words went down like a lead bullet and they insisted they drive the children to him. I was firm, pleading with them that my children would be disturbed and traumatised being driven away in this manner. I was handing them over calmly as requested, without a fight for their sake and appealed again that they allow the children's father to come to the house. There was no getting through and an intensity of cruelty built up as one car drove away to collect the car seats from Jonathan's car, and I sat on the pavement with Harry, Annie and Alfred waiting for its return.

Agony still rushed through my body and unaware whether I was in labour or losing the baby, I lifted Alfred closer to me, my heavy, solid little boy who clung to me desperately, crying uncontrollably. Annie was simultaneously pleading with me to let them stay. Harry remained silent, as the full implication of the events unfolded in his mind. He was being taken away again and all that I had been telling him had not been true. He was not protected and it could all happen again, and his life was not safe from the uncertainty he had lived through before. We waited huddled up together for what seemed like ages and it tormented us all that we would have to say goodbye in this way when the car returned. It was a slow motion, cruel parting and one that surely went against the basic human rights that we were all entitled to. A mother and her young children were being separated as she was potentially in labour; or worse still losing the baby that she had carried for a long nine months. Three children were being ripped from the mother they loved and needed, and a home that had finally become safe. It felt violent and desperately inhumane, watched by silent friends and neighbours, who could not take in the awfulness of the events that were unfolding in front of their eyes.

The police car returned. I strapped my dear Harry and Annie and Alfred in, and I locked into the desperation in their eyes, helpless and unable to protect my three beautiful children. I knew that this image of them all was imprinted on my mind and would never leave for as long as I lived. The car drove away, eyes still fixed on me out of the windows and for the first time since the November hearing six months ago, I completely broke down. I screamed a cry that echoed through the streets and I howled and howled; a keening coming out of the core of my being. I held the bump that was tight with pain; my baby. I feared I was losing the baby and I could do nothing to stop the pain or the tightening that occurred. There was no relief. Katie, Susy, Maria and Laura stood by and watched as there was nothing anyone could have done.

CHAPTER FOURTEEN

The next day there was a knock on the door and Social Services arrived, I thought at last to explain the actions of the previous day. Again I was wrong.

I had been left in an obvious state of shock as friends who stayed into the early hours of the morning eventually returned home and I fought in a desperate attempt to hang on to the little life inside me, for fear that something had gone wrong. I had to continue to self-anesthetise myself in my mind, to keep hold of my baby and not lose it, through the pain that gripped my body; sharp stabbing pains in my uterus which I could not recognise as normal. I had to go deep into my spiritual being and go to a place I had not known before. The sight of yet another unknown social worker at my door who followed me into my home was not what I had needed at that time. Even less so were the words she spoke, which were nothing other than untimely and reflected the lack of fairness I had received from Social Services throughout this journey. Despite the verdict of the courts I would always be guilty in their eyes.

She fiercely introduced herself as Carol Blasor, a new social worker, and spoke to me in a way that was both cold and unfriendly. Without a moment to waste she pointed a finger at my bump and inhumanely spoke of its imminent removal:

> *"The minute you give birth to that baby we will put it into care; you will not take your baby home. Be very careful about doing anything stupid as we will be watching you from now on. The minute you go into labour we will be advised and we will be waiting for you at Kingston Hospital."*

With that she left.

My solicitor began to unravel the events of the past 24 hours. It was directed, managed and controlled, unsurprisingly again by my husband, who was the train driver of this express, travelling at a thousand miles an hour, to a destination that would seemingly never arrive. Would he stop at nothing? Was there no one who would see through what appeared to be obsessed behaviour, displayed in such ruthless conduct? If anyone around me had been in any doubt about my performance as a mother, or questioned what had been going on behind closed doors, what had recently displayed in the last two days revealed it all. I had never made a public statement about my husband, nor had I betrayed our marriage in the community, but the way he had just treated me and his three children said everything. It reflected his deep inability to step into the shoes of his children and see the consequences of his actions on these vulnerable lives. Moreover it identified the lengths he would go to, to try and break me, using the children as necessary to achieve his goal.

As evidence began to unravel we discovered what instigated the children's abrupt removal, in circumstances of such barbarity. Firstly, Jonathan had persuaded the Cassel Hospital report to be sent to his solicitor only, not to both parties as per the court order. Secondly, he had taken it to the High Court that same day, to a new judge who had no knowledge of the preceding case at the Court of Appeal. Without presenting the court bundle or case history he successfully argued the necessity for the immediate removal of the children.

Keen therefore to see the contents of the Cassel Hospital report, Emily responded quickly to get hold of a copy, to try and identify on what basis the ruling had been made. Although shocking to read, the Cassel report reflected what my intuition had attested to only a few weeks earlier. It was a sad, yet clear demonstration of the voice and influence that both Dr Harwell and the O'Shea family had with all the service providers. The Cassel team stated that they 'broadly' agreed with Dr Harwell's claim that I suffered from Borderline Personality Disorder. It also said that the children should reside with their father. Dr Kimberly, who had never met me, signed his name to the report.

The court transcript revealed that Judge Holmes, who had been responsible for hearing the case, questioned why she had to deal with it on an ex parte basis; with the mother unaware that it had been presented to court and also being heavily pregnant. The response from Jonathan's solicitor was the Cassel report stated that when the mother eventually received a copy and realised that it was against her, there was a substantial threat of her, *attempting suicide and harming the children.*

Jonathan's legal representative went on to ask for direction from the court explaining to the judge what they wanted to happen. His solicitor stated that they envisaged the father would take the report to Social Services and the Child Protection team. He would then go to the local police station, so that they could be present together with Social Services when the children were collected from the mother. They also advised the judge that if Social Services had serious concerns for her, then the Child Protection Team may have to section her there and then.

This angered me hugely, because it went decidedly against how I had indeed reacted; being evidence in itself of the distortion and exaggeration of the truth presented in front of the judge. Worse however than the accusations made about me, was the corresponding wording that backed up the statement. The information was not based on me, or anything I had done or had said. It was heavily weighted on a printed statistic similar to the one Dr Harwell had submitted as 'evidence' right at the very beginning:

> *"...completed suicide occurs in 8 to 10 per cent of such individuals, and self mutilative acts are often a reason that these individuals present for help. The self-destructive acts are usually precipitated by threats of separation or rejection."*

In responding, the judge awarded the interim residence order back to the father but not before stating it was a very 'draconian' step to take.

Jonathan, the father to my four children, had been at the birth of the previous three and commented on each occasion, nothing other than what an extraordinary mother I had been. In fact he had always praised my parenting skills. However he was now capable of getting a Child Protection Order and removing them all from me. Although untrue, he depicted that an *'apparent likelihood'* of me hearing bad news could trigger suicide and went on to push all boundaries and actually have the children removed. Not only would he *not* support me as other husbands might, but neither would he protect me from hearing bad news; the very thing that might save my life! Maybe he hoped he could truly 'send me over the edge' and finally have me sectioned! I felt I could take little more.

The immediate effect of the ex parte order was my children being taken from me and their home that very same day, without me even being told as to why. This also meant my unborn child was to be removed as soon as it was born, despite the fact the courts still had no confirmation of any mental illness, nor evidence of harm to the children whom I so loved and had cared for these past six months alone.

I was now on the phone to my solicitor Emily, who had called because she was going to respond to the ex parte hearing. She needed to write an affidavit to the court and wanted me to go through the Cassel report with a fine tooth comb. She had to present a case to not only prove the judge had been wrong in removing the children, but wanted to expose the writings of the report as being unreliable and untrustworthy.

I sat down and read the long Cassel document and my stomach churned as I did so. It was difficult to decipher, because although it complimented the way I interacted with my children, I could see it then bent these observations to fit in with what they wished to say. It was clear that the author was trying to fit what had been witnessed into a report with preconceived guidelines. It was severe in its assessment of me, twisting normal, everyday child's play into accusations of neglect. For example, when Harry and Annie chose to play with the tea set and I engaged them by asking if they were making a cup for me tea for me, the therapist wrote describing how I expected them to 'look after me', mentioning that this was their role in relation to me. It essentially was suggesting that by asking the children to make me tea through role play, that my mental health state demanded the same in real life.

Although it quoted me favourably in most instances, it then went on to doubt that what they saw was genuine. A positive note would read that I displayed a great deal of skill and creativity in interacting with the children, describing how I was enthusiastic with praise for their achievements and showing much imagination in my attempts to involve them in both practical tasks and play. It highlighted my ability to handle sibling rivalry with competence and mentioned that the children had a lot to gain from this type of parenting. However this would be followed by raising a concern that I could not possibly maintain this type of stimulation or engagement. They made it clear that what they saw did *not* reflect what they had read already in the evidence submitted previously by my husband, mentioning that the rosy picture that they witnessed seemed to be rather at odds with the family dramas they had been reading about 'in the papers released to them', which could have only come from his corresponding with Social Services or Dr Harwell.

Highlighting the dichotomy of extremes, they commented on how the nurses interpreted my personality to be both 'powerful' and 'competent' suggesting I was a very capable teacher. However that was dismissed as, "*controlling.*"

The report stated that I made no effort to come to their level physically, yet I had sat on the floor, uncomfortable in the latter stages of pregnancy, as I cuddled them and they clung to me.

The report described how 'superficially' the time they spent observing my husband with the children compared poorly to the time they had spent with me in the same situation. They stated very clearly that it was 'worse' for the children because they were more unsettled and upset whilst with him, but instead of picking up on the truth behind 'why', they went on to say it revealed a more 'real' show of their feelings.

Categorically it stated that the children in my care revealed no sign of grave psychological disturbance, neither too did the team see any area where they saw risk arising to the children in my presence. In fact they could pick up on no faults to my parenting. Furthermore the team documented that it had to be stressed that I was encouraging, interested and involved with my children throughout all the sessions and was full of praise for their various achievements. They went on to say I had numerous positive skills which obviously reflected on many years of teaching and was fun, lively and imaginative. I clearly loved the children and they could find no fault that was 'necessarily conscious' during their sessions.

By contrast, regarding Jonathan they noted they were left with question marks as to how much he could be in touch with his children, with their feelings and with identifying with their suffering or needs. They listed many concerns: that he could not let the children speak; that Harry directed severe anger towards his father as well as impatience at his loss of control; that Jonathan avoided conflict through passive aggression; that he was unreliable; that he was in denial of his contribution in exasperating problems; that sibling rivalry occurred frequently in his presence; that he could not handle sibling rivalry; that Harry made it clear he wanted a stronger father who could deal with conflict; that the team witnessed inappropriate behavior in the room.

Regarding my husband's family, I read, interestingly, how Jonathan described his brother researching the hospital in detail— causing me to wonder why he would need to display this level of involvement in the affairs of our family. It was revealing also in describing how Jonathan's mother had been a Child Protection manager and had been the backbone behind his mission. The team clearly understood her role as being the catalyst propelling him to take action and confirmed that she knew Dr Harwell through her work. Furthermore it used Jonathan's own words describing her as 'formidable and vulnerable and frighteningly forceful'. It suggested too that Jonathan's passive aggressive nature presented as a denied ability to speak in her presence.

Most despicable was the fact that the Cassel report 'broadly' agreed with Dr Harwell. He had been heavily criticised by Lord Thornton in the Court of Appeal and Jonathan's legal team were advised he was not to be involved in the case. Yet following the hearing my husband had obviously given Dr Harwell's report to the Cassel, or they would not have known of his writings! Worse still, the Cassel report did not comment on what their findings were based on. Nowhere in the whole report, did their statement that I had BPD relate to any evidence regarding my behaviour, explain why the diagnosis was made, or establish what manifested in my personality to suggest I should be labelled with this disorder. All quotes about the 'illness' were in italics and sourced from a document or journal about the condition of a patient, rather than about me.

It was also recorded that Dr Kimberly retained final clinical responsibility for all work, but he had never met with any of us through the three month assessment period, even though he was court appointed. Why then was his report based on what he had 'read' as opposed to what he should have assessed?

Having finished reading the report I could only provide a critical summary for Emily. I emailed her the details, but concluded by saying the influence of Dr Harwell was abhorrent and the absence of Dr Kimberly was negligent. The Cassel Hospital's misrepresentation had led to this harrowing distortion of the truth chronicled in the latest document which had been used in court to remove my children for the second time.

CHAPTER FIFTEEN

By this stage neighbours and friends had witnessed for themselves the disturbing conduct of the professional services, by being present when they removed the children from me. The very people who were meant to protect both my family and I had failed us miserably once again, shamefully revealing another miscarriage of justice. Social Services had not bothered to visit or carry out any assessments during the past six months. In fact they had not even knocked on the door once, preferring to stay away rather than involve themselves with the children, whose safety they had been so concerned about. If friends had any doubt as to my innocence before, it became blindingly obvious to those around me, that I had been caught in a web of malfeasance. The mutual co-operation between these institutions ensured the system could be manipulated and justice had been prevented. Not only did the services appear to grant each other reciprocal recognition, but each one I assumed was not going to bring into disrepute the harmony and regularity that was afforded between them all.

The demonstrable negligence that had been illustrated, involved co-operation between Social Services, Dr Harwell working independently in private practice and more recently the Cassel had been added to the list of offenders. All had been so preoccupied by what Mr O'Shea and his family had been saying, that no one took the time to investigate his state of mental health and the drastic impact that his behaviour was having on the children. On the one hand I wondered how much further down the track I could go before the truth would be exposed. Yet on the other, my situation in the court was very different from criminal law, where I would have been innocent until proved guilty. In family law once the accusation had been made against me, it was becoming evident that I was clearly guilty until I proved myself innocent. Furthermore in criminal law, two sides of an argument are presented, but here I was legally prevented from making allegations about my husband's drinking and associated behaviour. The case was documented against me and it was up to me to prove my innocence.

Unless I was able to provide evidence that I did not suffer from Borderline Personality Disorder (which incidentally many people are diagnosed with and remain very capable of looking after their children) then any assumptions or indictments made about me were ostensibly accepted as the truth. This was the case, even though there was no evidence other than that provided unethically by a private doctor, with whom I had never registered as a patient, and a second doctor who had never met me, but whom had been drawn in by the first. Then adding the icing to the cake, was the fact that Social Services were working with no information other than both of their reports, that were handed to them on a silver platter by my husband and his family who had a vested interest in ensuring my children were removed.

I found myself in an absurd situation, becoming more accepting by the day that I would be unable to prove my innocence. The expert witnesses being used in court were brought in by solicitors, barristers and judges who, being 'independent', had never been involved in my life or that of the children. My family doctor was writing moving reports of her admiration of my role as a mother and the bond between the children and I, stating that she was personally deeply affected by the removal of the children, but her report was not allowed to be used. My health visitor who had seen me with all my babies and visited me regularly both at home and in the surgery, was also not allowed to submit evidence to the court. The effect of this impacted her so severely, that she had to leave her current position and move to another practice, because she had become 'overly concerned' and 'too emotionally involved'.

The teachers, nursery helpers, shop keepers, dentist, milkman, the neighbours who had seen us daily for the past four years were not allowed to articulate or communicate to the court what they all knew and had seen. The only people allowed to comment were those who were paid huge sums of money for their services, but whom remained apparently clueless as to the truth of what they were saying, or biased towards the articulate words of my husband.

With all this going on and the fear of the unknown looming, my mind played havoc with the awareness of Social Services' intervention before me. I wanted to get on a plane and disappear somewhere safe to deliver my baby, where no one could take it away but it was too late to fly. Also my suggestion to Emily that I go to Ireland quickly did not go down well. I had been warned by Social Services not to do anything silly, and sense spoke to me that they would likely track me down there, or anywhere else I should choose to escape. I felt a helplessness and an inability to protect my unborn baby, who had so far survived the stress of the past tumultuous nine months and I longed to be free from danger.

Following a similar pattern to my other three pregnancies, I guessed I was now in the second day of a slow labour. Unlike my friends who seemed to produce babies quickly, I knew that this would take time. As contractions strengthened, my sister arrived and we shed tears together as I voiced how I had been denied my only chance of delivering at home. Laura was training as a midwife at the time, and with my fourth child I would loved to have climbed into a bath and chill with her around. It would have been a blessing to welcome the district midwife to help me deliver in the comfort of my own home for the first time. I could think of nothing nicer than to have been able to return to sleep in my own inviting bed afterwards, with the crisp white sheets I had recently ironed. Nor too could I have wanted more than having friends and neighbours around that I somehow depended on. The community felt safe, secure and impregnable and it was them that had made it so.

Instead, we drove the route through the streets of Ham, to Kingston Hospital, ironically built on the site of the former Kingston Union Workhouse as a result of the Poor Amendment act in 1834. The bumpy road reminded me of the delicate path I now trod as we parked and entered the maternity building, being greeted courteously upon our arrival. Supporting me as a sister, Laura quickly and assertively stepped into a mother role, as she walked me to the room I was to stay for the challenging next few days of this precipitous journey. She was a rock by my side encouraging me at every moment through the physical, mental and emotional fear I felt. Social Services had already been in contact with the hospital and had organised my isolation in an area where I could be monitored and watched. It was into that delivery room, away from the main ward, that Laura brought a real sense of peace.

How she endured through the unknown outcome of the labour, without being supported herself I still don't know, but if ever there was an angel by my side it was her right then. She had been at the birth of Alfred less than two years ago and I knew having her with me again would get me through. She was strong when I was weak; she was hopeful when I was fearful; calm when I was shouting and encouraging when I wanted to give up as the pain grew unbelievably strong. She wiped me with soothing flannels, massaged my feet, held my shaky arms in hers, gave me small sips of water and kept me up to date with the progress I was making. She could have done nothing more if she had tried. Love oozed through the pores in her skin and I thought of our own dear mother and how proud she would have been. She would have been so honoured to watch her youngest daughter hold together the birth of her last grandchild and I felt her spirit there with us both, as though she needed to make her presence known.

The midwife was a sweet young girl and the two of them got on well, gently sharing a few stories, which were a welcome distraction through the strength of the contractions, pulling my body into birth. Together they encouraged me and supported me, with an appropriate variation between laughter and a serious professional approach in handling the imminent delivery. They were a highly impressive team, even managing to escort Social Services out of the room, when they appeared at the worst stage of labour. It was to my great delight that they stated that their timing was highly inappropriate and told them they could wait.

It wasn't a quick delivery but soon I held the most beautiful baby girl in my arms, weighing just a little over seven pounds. The room filled with rays of love and joy that were tangible. I named her Alice Rose. The children had chosen Alice, and she had always been described as a rose that would bring new life and renewed hope in the depth of such darkness—and she did. This was a little girl who had voyaged with me, surviving the last nine months of fear, pain, anguish, deep suffering and loss. When the other children had gone, she had remained with me and together we had journeyed along.

Together we had fought for their return and together we had got to this stage where I held her in my arms and cried, as the others were no longer able to share in this moment of such great joy. This little girl was tough, she was a survivor and she had managed to make it through.

I yearned to share this minute with Harry and Annie and Alfred who had been so excited, expectantly hoping to see their little sister emerge into their lives. We had spent many hours planning what we would call the baby; discussing how she would arrive, how they would hold her and what we could do to welcome her into our little family. There was an enormous triumph in dear little Alice's appearance, but the loss of the other three stole the complete euphoria that I should have felt at that time.

I knew that the children had been told of her delivery as Social Services had contacted Jonathan to break the news and announce her name. The loss of my beautiful children, and the extent of their own suffering—still really so little themselves—made me break down and the tears sprinted down my cheeks onto Alice's tiny feet. Their little photos adorned my room, pictures of them laughing and giggling and looking so adorable were everywhere I looked. I ached to have them sitting on my bed and was desperate to hold them, reassuring their confusion and imagined rejection, with my arms tucked around them all. Instead of which I was without them and everything made me cry as I lay on my bed, cleaned up from the birth and suckling Alice on my breast. The thought that I was unable to go home as I had with the others, was hard to accept, as was the sunny day outside that I was not allowed to see, other than through a tiny window in my room.

The music playing in the private rooms beside me and the sight of fathers visiting their wives and bringing in their children brought home the finality that things had turned out the way they had. They were reminders too highlighting that I would never again have this moment to share Alice with the siblings who should have been there but weren't. The ghastly food and the watchful nurses triggered loneliness as did the presence of Social Services and the memories; so many haunting echoes which were so nauseatingly fresh in my mind.

Social Services came in and interviewed me. I said yes and no in all the right places as I had always done before, but not quite knowing anymore what the right places actually were. Was I depressed? Was I tired? Was I feeling emotional? There was a long list of ridiculous questions that actually I wasn't safe to answer as I knew whatever I said would be wrong.

Later I saw how astute my assumptions were, as I listened to suggestions that if I was holding Alice I was obsessed with the baby and if my sister was holding her I hadn't bonded. I had to fit into assessment boxes and I could see frustration on the face of the social workers if they couldn't get the right tick in the correct place on their form. I watched as facial expressions would change and I was discerning enough not to give them anything they could work on. They were potentially dangerous people and I felt judgmental and patronising in every way, and I wanted them out of my room and away from my bonding time with Alice. They had stolen so much from me and they wanted to occupy this treasured time with the birth of my fourth child, but I wasn't going to let them.

My last two deliveries were also at Kingston Hospital maternity ward, but as the beds were in high demand I was out, and back at home as fast as I could be sent. This time however it was not permissible for me to leave; I had to be watched and monitored and was not allowed to vacate my room. Even though the sun shone outside on a beautiful mid-June English afternoon, my boundary was the room door and as much as I ached for Alice to breathe her first fresh summer's air, it was not to be.

Laura and Maria barely left my side for the next few days and I was blessed tremendously by wonderful visitors who arrived like a gently flowing river, appearing at perfectly planned intervals so I was never left alone.

Katie and Susy my dear 'sister' friends were there as soon as they could get permission to come. They breezed in with a wicker hamper of food and gifts for Alice, wrapped in tissue paper and little pink ribbons. They had also kept my allotment going the last few days, watering the plants and picking the vegetables and flowers that had all appeared in a sudden harvest. As if to show their allegiance they had blossomed early, wanting I was sure, to be involved also in the euphoria of the moment. In the hamper they had brought me the sweet peas, their pleasant aroma smelling of the hours of labour the children and I had toiled on the land and their fragrance drifted into the air to disguise the disinfectant smell in the ward. Friends from church brought laughter into the room. Some sang songs, whilst others prayed and there never seemed a moment when someone wasn't turning up, calling, or delivering a card or a gift for Alice. My room became adorned with bouquets of every colour and presents filled any surface that was bare.

Alice slept and woke and fed, and we gazed at each other for endless hours, her eyes focussing sooner, I was sure, than the others had ever done. I was convinced she knew, as I did, that there was a bond between us that no one could steal no matter what else had been taken from us both. There were moments I cried with those around me and moments we laughed, but most of the time we had so many questions to ask, as we all remained aghast at what had so recently taken place. We could barely bring to our lips the awfulness of what Alice's sister and brothers would be enduring as separation had taken place in such a startling and unexpected manner. Nor could we imagine the despair that must have been occupying every part of their being, at such a young age.

The kindness I was shown in the midst of such worry for my other children marked an extreme I had never known. At one end of the scale I faced the fear that troubled my children which I learnt later would only serve to open up the old wounds that had just started to heal. These recent events would cause their old scars to rip open with an inhumane fierceness laying them exposed to further pain that would haunt them for years to come and undo any imaginable healing that might have already started to take place.

At the other end of the spectrum however, was a love being demonstrated to me that I had also never known. A cousin who had worked with Mother Teresa for years in Calcutta, who wore no shoes in England and lived in poverty himself, as he served others, came to visit. Touchingly he hugged me goodbye as he left and handed me a small brown envelope which he slipped into my fingers, before winking, transferring a ray of hope onto me. Inside the envelope there were two hundred, twenty pound notes, tied together with an elastic band. Under a little picture of Mother Teresa, he had written the words: "Giving isn't giving, unless you give in love, until it hurts". I knew he had nothing left.

Another friend handed me the first ten per cent of her husband's new bonus. Homemade meals arrived and I felt held and supported in a way I would never have believed possible. Most importantly to me, I was never alone when Social Services visited. It brought me great assurance to be in a position where they felt unable to humiliate me as they had done so many times in the past when I faced them unaccompanied. Their influence was somehow diminished when others were around, and I vowed to myself that I would never again underestimate the emotional and psychological abuse that is experienced by the vulnerable from those holding positions of power.

I had witnessed this materialising so many times by people in professional organisations. I had been exposed to staff who belittled me and patronised me, when I had already been stripped of my basic human rights, being left in a position of such weakness that I was only able to comply with all being done to me and said at me. I realised importantly from my situation, how one can be empowered by the love of others in the presence of such animosity. It revealed to me how low I had previously sunk, where I simply accepted abuse as the norm, to the degree I molded into giving in to what was too exhausting to fight.

CHAPTER SIXTEEN

It was on the fifth day that a well-dressed gentleman who I did not recognise entered my room and introduced himself as the hospital psychiatrist. He had been sent by Social Services to interview me and assess me for their reports. He called himself Mark. Considerately, he asked my permission if he could sit and took the time to shake hands with me explaining politely what his role was. His positive demeanour struck me; I was impressed with his gentleness, calculating instantly he was a good, kind man. He told me a little of his background having previously been a vicar in the church and he exuded compassion as he spoke. I felt quickly drawn to this fatherly man who I understood could be trusted, and whom to this very day I both honour and owe deep gratitude for bringing a turning point to the downhill ride I had been on.

I knew the questions that he would soon be asking as I had

answered them on three previous occasions; at the Richmond Hamlet Hospital; at The Priory and with the team at the Cassel Hospital. Now on the fourth occasion, if I didn't yet know the psychiatric assessment inside out then I would have indeed been as crazy as my husband was trying to allege. Not only did I know the questions, but I could have probably recited them in the same order, back to front and probably upside down too. One by one he asked them and one by one I responded.

There was only one question I pondered in my mind and had to pause and reflect on, "Have you ever had suicidal intentions?" The truth was I had never wanted to kill myself and had never thought of doing so, but how could I admit that when all hope was gone and I had lost my children that I didn't want to die? It was a ridiculous question. Who would not have wanted to die when they had lost their three small children through injustice in the family courts? But the answer was 'no'. I guess the evidence that I was still alive through what I had endured was proof in itself that I was strong enough to make it through. No way were my children ever to lose the mother who had brought them into the world, when she loved them so much, and they needed her more than ever.

To avoid looking like I already knew the drill, I paused at times to ponder the question. As I did so, I became aware that I enjoyed playing the system, while I hesitated in answering, as though I had never been asked these questions before. I knew the criteria for Borderline Personality Disorder. I knew the symptoms of; a manic depressive, a schizophrenic, a psychotic, a pyromaniac, a hypochondriac; a neurotic and for phobias, anxiety disorders and depressives. As I considered what I had been exposed to since this whole nightmare had begun, I suddenly understood how someone could be so easily pushed into one of these disorders, by society and its treatment of individuals. I knew also that I was lucky; I had not actually broken under the pressure, which could so easily have launched me into any one of the above.

I laughed in my head as I remembered the words of my brother-in-law, who just yesterday had come to visit especially to coach me, knowing that I had this interview ahead. In our one hour session which he conducted like a business meeting, he advised me brilliantly that I should not exaggerate when interviewed, or be too sensitive or too unemotional. He suggested that I should not discuss low points, but be positive, thoughtful and take time to consider each question, without rushing to a response and without seeming overly knowing. He was an excellent encourager and as the questions flowed from the psychiatrist, I heard Peter's voice behind me inspiring me on, and I considered his response and how he would have delivered it. I knew as well that I should not only focus on the exhaustive list of questions that this man had to work through. I targeted my attention also on Alice, who he had already admired and I paused him as she woke and asked if he minded me feeding her. Not only was I keen to do so, but also wanted to make sure he could not write in his report that I was unable to focus on her needs. I was hyper-alert in a way that was not in my nature but necessary for the task at hand. It was part of what the process of the past nine months had taught me.

At the same time as being aware of the game I played, I enjoyed enormously Mark's company, who brought a touch of human empathy to the world of psychiatry that I had not yet seen and indeed a lightness and peace to my room too. I admired his skill in relaxing me and ensuring I felt safe, which I did. I wondered what kind of husband he would be to his wife and felt slightly jealous that other women could be treated kindly by men they had chosen to marry, when mine was intent on seeing me end up in a mental institution, with my children being removed from my side.

It dawned on me the affliction to which I had become not only subjected to, but also the degree to which I had become accustomed to it. I wondered if Mark would think the behaviour uncommon practice for a husband whose wife had just delivered his child. It suddenly appalled me that it took this kind gentleman to remind me of how men had a responsibility to behave. I had become so familiar with hearing about what I was doing wrong, that I had forgotten that as a mother and a wife, I had felt no support, respect, trust or love from the man I had married as I tried to raise our family.

Mark had played no power games and appeared to have no hidden agenda as had been the norm with everyone I had met in Social Services and at the Cassel Hospital. He was a man of honour who brought back integrity into the profession within which he worked. I felt gratitude that he would have access to some of the most vulnerable people in our society, who I understood deserved so badly, to be handled professionally and shown compassion during their care.

Mark questioned and chatted to me for a lengthy two and a half hours before concluding his interview. My expectation was for him to leave to later discover my fate through reading his report second hand, after it had been passed on to the relevant authority. Instead however, he mentioned he was very moved and touched by the day's interview and troubled deeply by the story I had disclosed. He said he felt compelled to take a quiet hour to write up his notes and present them to me, so that I could read them and comment before he passed them on to anyone and ahead of any other eyes reading them through.

He took the time to say that he admired my strength in fighting for the return of my children through what appeared to be a series of injustices. He showed empathy and understanding at my anguish and spoke with confident authority against much that I had been exposed to. He expressed that he desired to see me reunited with my children so that they could enjoy the relationship he had witnessed between Alice and I which was so obviously apparent. He continued by saying he did not wish to add to any distress by keeping confidential what he was to report.

Sure enough, he stood by his word and he returned an hour

later. His document in hand, he passed it to me to read. His writing opened by detailing the referral:

"Social Services requesting assessment, prior to patient going home c/o Child, Alice (newly born)."

He stated:

"On assessment (and in agreement with patient's GP, Dr Kotella, with whom I later spoke) I could discern nothing to suggest Mrs O'Shea has a Borderline Personality Disorder nor any other form of psychiatric disorder; ward staff reported her behaviour with Alice as exemplary. She handled her with love and tenderness throughout the assessment—and verbally expressed nothing to suggest she is anything other than a loving and caring mother going through a nightmare experience as a result of claims made either by her husband, his mother or their confidantes. She expresses confidence in her legal team, is well supported by her friends and local church, and expressed her desire to regain custody of her children not to win a battle with her husband, not to prove a point, but overwhelmingly for what she considers the children's future well-being. In summation, no psychiatric issues apparent, no concerns re safety of patient or dependents in her care."

A discharge of water emptied from my tear ducts and poured down my cheeks as I perused the complimentary observations he had made during our interview. The report was to the point; clear and concise and I felt a warmth rise within me as I realised there was nothing that could be used against me, even if one tried to reinterpret or twist the words that were in front of my eyes.

What struck me was that this would really upset Social Services because at this time they had involved themselves without any substantial reason to do so. They had no evidence whatsoever that would even hint that they should be involved with me, and were clawing desperately to fill their files with anything more than accusations made by the O'Shea family. So far they had nothing on me and obviously were worried, and they had every right to be so. I was not going to let them get away with what they had done. I was beginning to comprehend—as much as I sensed they were—that they had picked on the wrong person. My resolve to fight had been propelled to a new level of intensity.

Mark's report not only cleared my name but lifted my spirits restoring truth back into my life. I was a good mother! I was of sound mind, intelligent, motivated, not disturbed or manifesting symptoms of mental illness. At no time did I display any of the ten Borderline Personality Disorder criteria. It felt good to read my strengths and qualities on paper and rediscover that I was likable, interesting and fun to be with. I felt reassured that I could place confidence in the 'professionals' once again and hope this would lead to a new, positive outcome, with doors opening in the future, rather than closing.

I thanked him sincerely before he left and felt a huge peace come over me, which I enjoyed with Alice as I held her and contemplated with optimism into her future.

While I had been in hospital my solicitor had returned to court as planned to contest the 'ex parte' order which, in Latin, means 'on one side only,' or 'for one party,' and occurs when only one side is present in court without the other. The absent party is then given a limited number of days to appeal a court ruling, submitting evidence and requesting the decision made by a judge be reviewed. In this situation, my husband submitted documentation without us being represented and so Emily put forward our case for the children's return. In doing so she conveyed to the court the proposal for the possible discharge of the mother from hospital by Social Services.

In revising the case, Judge Holmes recognised and expressed her disquiet that she had not been fully informed on 3rd June. She was disturbed that she had not known of Lord Thornley's ruling, nor had she been presented with the full evidence from the case history. She acknowledged that she had made a ruling based on the Cassel report. Now however, she expressed she saw the case in a new light, having seen the Kingston Hospital psychiatric report, which, in agreement with the views of the mother's General Practitioner, raised no concerns.

This she discussed along with the Local Authority's agreement to discharge both mother and Alice home; the positive reports from the midwife visits; the home and surgery visits from Dr Kotella; the visits from the health visitor; and the visits from the social worker, both announced and unannounced. Having established that none of the visits resulted in any action being taken, or concern being expressed, she concluded that the mother was able to care for the children. She described how the ex parte application had been irregular and unsatisfactory; especially as she did not have her attention drawn to the father's endeavours, nor the response of the Court of Appeal to his actions in the recent past. She highlighted how the Cassel report was now seen as controversial. Firstly because of the diagnosis of Borderline Personality Disorder which she claimed to some extent was a derivative of Dr Harwell's assumptions. Secondly, because of the recommendation that there should be long-term placement of the children with the father.

Beyond that she discussed how the 'perceived' emergency risk of suicide and harm to the children from the mother had not occurred, despite the extraordinary stresses that she was placed under by taking the children from her care. She immediately discharged the interim residence order from the father but did not return the children.

She adjourned the application to be heard by a High Court judge. Whilst she could not bring the children home, she could order a full hearing to be heard in a few days' time, which would decide the children's fate.

CHAPTER SEVENTEEN

Whilst my legal team were in the throes of court proceedings, Social Services with the latest psychiatric assessment in hand had consented to my leaving hospital and returning back to Kings Road and the warmth of where I longed to be. However, they forced me to sign an agreement with them before I was allowed to leave the maternity ward. This meant that I would remain under their watchful eye with various written terms and conditions that included not leaving the house without previously informing them:

> *"Mrs O'Shea will inform and discuss with Social Services of any plans to leave her home address even on a temporary basis."*

Regretfully, and naively, I signed the document not realising that they had no legal right to be involved with my family or me at that time. Later, I perceived I was manipulated through my ignorance as I had no idea what I should add my name to, nor did I know what my rights actually were. I wondered how many families were in worse situations than me and had lost their children to foster care or even forced adoption, through making decisions whilst remaining oblivious of their legal standing. The power this organisation wielded became more evident as time elapsed. I began to have a greater understanding of how parents would sign their children away for one reason only, and that was fear.

Another condition attached to returning home with Alice was that I agreed to an emergency child protection conference a few days later at the offices of Twickenham Social Services. They wanted to place Alice on the child protection register and I guessed if they managed to do so, their files would carry more weight. So far they still had nothing on me other than the previous allegations made by my husband and his family and this was probably a chance for them to document negative findings from the professionals, who had been associated with our lives.

I had barely given birth to Alice, was breastfeeding my fourth child and surviving without a husband, when I had to endure unwelcome questioning in a formal Social Services meeting room not far away. I returned with trepidation to the offices I had visited eight months earlier and entered a room monopolised by an enormous, highly polished conference table. Already seated were those people who were there to give evidence. It was another frightening situation, highlighting my isolation from the sense of normality displayed in the lives of those around me. It also brought back to the fore all I had been subjected to. Wounds of betrayal and injustice opened up and teardrops blubbered their way down my cheeks falling onto Alice's little face as I sat and held her tight in my arms. She was only a few days old and I wished I could have been anywhere else with her than here. With my other children I would by this stage be walking with their prams in the park, picnicking with friends and their children, or chilling with family, entertaining these precious moments of enjoying a new born baby.

There was an atmosphere of contention in the air in this intimidating room, and glancing over at Carol Blasor, as well as the other officers who were handling this case, did little to encourage my fragile presence. I felt vulnerable simply by being in the room.

Jonathan had asked to attend to give evidence but was fortunately prevented from doing so and it was a welcome relief on my part. A few days previously he had agreed through solicitors to bring Harry, Annie and Alfred to hospital to see me. He had requested to meet Alice but at the appointed time called to say he would not appear, explaining that it was, 'an obvious danger' for me to see my children. This had devastated me and I think Social Services realised it was not appropriate for him to be in the same room as me. I also had no desire to sit near him whilst having to face so intimidating a situation.

The meeting was formally opened and like a school-child being reprimanded I was spoken to by the presiding officer. Immediately, under 'Reasons for the Child Protection Conference,' he mentioned Borderline Personality Disorder. He discussed the background circumstances, the allegations against me, the removal of my children, my instability and the obvious need to place Alice under strict supervision. Carol Blasor reinforced his speech and spoke of her experience in cases like mine where the mother was mentally ill and the children were in need of proper care. As words emerged from her mouth I could do nothing to curtail the now running river of tears flooding both Alice and I. I was angry at myself for crying, as I thought it highlighted my weakness and vulnerability of which they spoke. I was also furious at the obvious power games they immediately played in manipulating and steering the conversation towards putting Alice on the register, when they had not yet heard any evidence. Even the 'Brief Chronology of Relevant Information,' contained only facts fed to Social Services by my husband and his family. Everything they had talked of had been based only on what my husband's family were saying, or the 'so called' evidence produced by Dr Harwell and the Cassel. It appeared they were speaking of this to only influence those in the room who would later vote.

I was astounded that they were still using mental illness as their justification, despite the absence of any evidence of it, ignoring their two formal assessments which denied the charge they had laid against me. I doubted whether any of the people sitting at the table would have survived all I had endured without cracking under pressure or turning to the bottle, or some other vice to get through all the system had thrown at me thus far.

As Carol finished speaking, the table was opened to discussion. The conversation passed round one by one, each presenting their evidence. We began with a report from my GP which was read in her absence. It described at length her close relationship with me; treating the children for common colds and illnesses and the investigation of my recurrent immune disorder symptoms that had not yet been resolved. It mentioned her supporting me through three pregnancies and her obstetric referrals to Kingston Hospital and described my ability to accept responsibility for resolving obvious difficulties within my marriage.

My GP's report discussed my vulnerability in the presence of my husband and revealed great sympathy for all she had been party to hearing in the past few months. She highlighted how this had upset not only her but the whole general practice who knew me well. They apparently had never been witness to Social Services become involved without assessing a family first and had responded with disturbance at the twice abrupt removal of the children. She pointed to the stress this would have caused and commented that it had been most unnecessary.

My GP questioned why Social Services had not contacted the practice if concerns had been raised. She had obviously taken time and careful consideration to write her thoughts. The report detailed the loving relationship with my children, the atmosphere of respect between us, the fun we had and the commitment I had made to motherhood in very lonely circumstances. Discussing the removal of the children she noted:

> *"Mrs O'Shea said that she was coping well on most days but occasionally did feel low. During the consultation she was tearful saying that at times she gets upset when she thinks of the other children. She was upset at what they may be thinking and had their Mummy stopped caring for them as she has now had a new baby and why did Mummy leave not saying goodbye to them. She is missing them very much but at the same time is trying hard to stay positive. I would describe her reactions and emotions as normal."*

Her report was followed by another written by my health visitor and read also in her absence. It described comparable observations and in addition commented on the pleasant atmosphere she always enjoyed entering our home where there was laughter, hugs and children sitting on my lap. She spoke of her distress at the children's removal, her inability to do anything to help and how this in turn had affected her employment in the practice.

She also mentioned that she had never witnessed such injustice in all her years as a health professional, nor had she seen any evidence as to why Social Services' intervention had been necessary. She asked the question why any of the professionals involved like the GP, herself, nursery teachers et cetera had not first been consulted if concerns had been raised:

"Additionally, in order to make sound judgements pertaining to the welfare of the children and family, it is imperative that communications amongst the relevant professionals are maintained and that and relevant information is shared."

It was certainly something that had not taken place so far and a pleasing smile crept over my face. I whispered to Alice that we would be okay, and not only were we were going to make it through but we would also see the return of her siblings.

If I had by this time stopped crying, I started again immediately when the next lady introduced herself as the police officer that accompanied Social Services to remove my children and was present at the house two weeks previously. She instantly broke down as she described the violation she felt when the order was handed to me and the children were removed. She described it as one of the most tranquil of homes and scenes she had entered with peace filling the house, happy children and a mother about to give birth. She explained how well I had handled the situation considering the stress I was under, and made the situation positive for the children by saying they were going to see their dad.

She went on to say how it went against everything she believed in, stating she had not slept well since and fearfully admitted the scene would haunt her for the rest of her life. Compassionately she looked at me and apologised for the distress she had personally caused by being present.

The Midwife who had delivered Alice made a straightforward positive statement and concluded by saying:

"During her stay in hospital Mrs O'Shea cared for the baby all the time and her attention and interaction with the baby is reported to be excellent. Mrs O'Shea continued

*to breast feed the baby very well and was able to meet all
of the baby's needs appropriately."*

Maria was another professional who had been asked to speak today.
Tragically though she had suffered a terrible bereavement, which
she had been absent from while she sat with me for a number of
days in hospital. She had to take some time out to grieve. In her
place came another representative from Victim Support who knew
me well. She took pleasure in delivering her evidence, supporting
and adding to what seemed to be the general consensus about both
my mental health and my ability to mother my children, as well
as mentioning what I had been through. She described the love I
displayed towards Alice and added:

*"This was one of the worst cases of psychological abuse
from a spouse Victim Support had seen."*

I was sad that Maria could not be with me to hear the evidence being
delivered, as she had suffered much in supporting me through the
last few months. She deserved to hear the vindication being released
in the conference, which confirmed all she had been speaking to
me. She had said on so many occasions that the truth would finally
come to light and it would all be resolved. Today in this austere
room in a town a little west of London her words were ringing true.

   In summing up, the presiding officer reminded members at the
conference that they were to consider how concerned they were for
Alice's welfare, and to decide if her name should be included on
Richmond's Child Protection Register. He started by saying:

*"The information to the conference in respect of Alice sug-
gests that Mrs O'Shea cares for her well and there is no
concern raised for her welfare. She is meeting all her devel-*

opmental milestones and her relationship with Mrs O'Shea
is seen to be strong. She has attended the conference with
her mother and seemed very comfortable in the meeting
despite the usual difficulty for parents in these meetings."

There was a stunned silence and a warmth overwhelmed my heart. Could this be a turning point? Could this be enough for Social Services to back off and leave me alone so I could have my children returned to me? If they did, it would be the first time for almost a year. An air of expectancy filled the room as the presiding officer opened the meeting up to a ballot.

The vote was whether to place Alice on the child protection register or not. It was a straight yes or no. My social worker Carol Blasor began the voting and to my surprise said:

"It is a particularly difficult decision to make, as I do not
wish to contribute to any further psychological distress
to Mrs O'Shea, which I have heard in the information
disclosed today."

She voted 'no'.

There followed a 'no' on behalf of my GP and a 'no' on behalf of my heath visitor. There was a 'no' from the police officer, a 'no' from Victim Support and a 'no' from the midwife. Then there followed a pause as we waited for the presiding officer to speak. My interpretation of the expression on his face led me to believe he was agitated and unsettled and I wondered what he would say. A silent interruption paused the moment and as all eyes glanced his way his mouth opened and uttered a quiet, amazing;

"Six nos."

Immediately there followed another even more hesitant pause:

"It is a unanimous decision not to place Alice on the child protection register."

I allowed a small smile to creep over my face for all to see, joined by the two lovely ladies sitting beside me who I could feel celebrating quietly inside. We glanced at each other and our relief met somewhere in the space between us. Peace suddenly descended in the building as though a vault in the ceiling had opened up, and harmony cascaded around Alice and me, as we looked into each other's eyes. Without a measure of doubt, truth had determined the outcome of the vote and I kissed my dear little Alice gently on her cheek before she briskly fell asleep.

Justice prevailed in the room that day and as I walked free from the watchful gaze of Social Services, I made sure I looked them in the eye as I walked past carrying Alice. She and I were to be left alone. Social Services no doubt would have to come to terms with not only empty files, but two psychiatric assessments of their own claiming no mental illness and now a documented meeting with real evidence minuted by their own fair hands. I was curious if they would look with new eyes at their communication with Jonathan, his family and Dr Harwell, and detect suspicion, or experience at least a small sense of doubt regarding all that filled their books. I felt their motives had been exposed—not to me as I knew it from the start—but glaringly to others who saw it staring them in the face. Social Services were the ones who had today invited everyone to witness for themselves the professional abuse that had occurred. I was driven home, a very happy lady. This was the outcome I needed to strengthen me to get through the next hurdle that would come my way. It restored some normality accompanied by a new level of enthusiasm, which allowed me to march ahead fighting for the right for my children to return home.

CHAPTER EIGHTEEN

It was the end of June and I had not seen Harry, Annie or Alfred for over three weeks. I knew from evidence being submitted to the court they were currently living in Guildford and that the children's grandparents had moved from Dorset to Surrey, to be closer to London. The stream of writing coming from my husband's solicitor revealed that arrangements had been made to ensure the children could live with them long term, as Jonathan would be able to commute to work from there. It broke my heart to hear how Harry had yet again been registered in a new school. It concerned me too how unsettling this would be for him, having only just recently adjusted back into our village primary school, before being hurried away yet again, with no preparation and no goodbye.

The abrupt removal of my children was incredibly damaging. Harry had not only lost the security of being with his mother, but aged six was facing his fourth school move in less than ten months. All three children were living in their sixth house move in the same space of time, disorienting them and causing deep rooted insecurity which would lead to extreme anxiety later on.

My heart broke as I read the evidence of the inappropriate arrangements that had been made for my children by their father and his parents. It overwhelmed me to think I had no right to protect them from damaging decisions that would have grave long term consequences on their development and well-being. Not having the children with me was one thing, but being denied one's basic instinct to protect them was a violation of my human rights as a mother.

Harry would usually rejoice in seeing me at the end of the school day, his whole face lighting up as he located me amongst the sea of mothers waiting at the classroom doors. He would call my name as he ran throwing himself into my arms as though we had been apart for weeks. He was an incredibly affectionate child and loved his cuddles, holding my hand wherever we went and sitting on my lap at any opportune moment when it had been vacated by the others. He was at such an inquisitive and interesting age. He loved anything three dimensional, making models at school from paper roll tubes and the remains of cereal packets, all taped together with whatever he could find. He had an affinity for towers and would build them in Lego or bricks and each one had a character individual to the other. He loved the outdoors too, preferring to dig holes on the allotment that could be filled with hose water and jumped in, to learning about the vegetables that were being replaced by the areas he had dug. He would ride his bike, being competent with balance from an early age and loved the freedom that cycling would bring as he peddled next to me, happy that he no longer had to walk.

Annie had just turned four. She had been enrolled in a new nursery, her fourth move in a short space of time. It was nearing the end of the academic year and I had been robbed of my last chance to be with her at home before she was to start school. It was such a precious time that we were sharing, as we used to walk to the infant school nursery at the end of our road, where we knew most of the children from the village and familiarity was of essence.

I had been in a National Childbirth Trust baby group whilst pregnant with Annie, alongside mothers who were all due around her expected birth date. Once our babies were born we all used to meet regularly at each other's houses. As we all chatted and counselled one another through the promptings of the day, our babies played as they crawled and then learnt to walk. We would gather four or five times a week at home, or at various little playgroups in church halls or clubs where we could grab a much desired cup of coffee, whilst we watched our offspring grow and fumbled around on deprived sleep that was so typical of life with small toddlers. The children of these mothers became close friends with Annie, but sadly in her absence they had formed close bonds with each other, which she was not part of. I felt a wave of sorrow that she was missing so much. The little of the year I had with her we played in the parks which were a few streets from our house. We visited the allotment to sow our seeds for the coming year, walked by the River Thames feeding the ducks with any leftover bread we could find, played on the swings and pushed Alfred in his buggy wherever we went. They were happy times and Annie was currently at an age where she adored doing 'mummy things,' from baking to sewing, to fashioning objects out of play dough, painting, and making anything she could, from whatever lay around. Like me she was creative and imaginative and obviously appreciated transforming things to look beautiful. She delighted in dressing up, laying tables and decorating the tops of fairy cakes we baked together, as her baby brother emptied the cupboards and drawers below.

Alfred was almost two with his birthday not far away. I had been denied most of his crawling months and missed his first steps, as well as many of the fascinating stages a toddler of this age develops through. Sadness hovered over me like a low drizzle of rain, from all those milestones that could never be retrieved, and instantly such loss filled me. I remembered how Alfred would sit on my hip for most of the day and more recently how he had clung to me during the last few months in an obvious desperation to not be separated again. He was a feisty little boy and showed no restraint at hiding his feelings. I knew that anger would be an issue for this beautiful little boy in later life, as a consequence of all that was confusing for him at this time.

Alfred loved his siblings, and as Annie 'mummied' him, Harry would give him toys but then quickly remove them with displeasure, as Alfred banged them or dropped them onto the floor. He would then cry to make his displeasure known; cleverly realising Annie would mediate between her brothers, playing fair and not seeing what the fuss was all about. I imagined the distress in the grandparents' house as tension would manifest in the children and so little assurance would come. I had already heard from Annie how she felt abandoned in her previous episode away, as she used to talk very openly about all that went on in her grandparents' house. She said repeatedly she hated her grandma and had told me frequently of crying for me but then being shut in her room or being scolded for screaming. I listened as she spoke often of the absence of love in their home.

Before their abrupt removal only a few weeks earlier they had been terribly excited at the imminent arrival of another sibling who they knew was a girl. They would stroke my bump, talk to the baby and even try to push it aside, as they contended for space on my ever diminishing lap. They had talked of being there when Alice was coming out, accepting that they would have to wait until she had actually been born to visit. They longed to be able to meet her, hold her and bring her the cards they had made. I knew after this period of time away they would be wondering why they had not seen her and why they were cruelly not allowed to see me. I struggled with the picture that they felt rejected and replaced as I held another child—Annie in particular—by another girl.

I contemplated how they had coped with their father's broken promise that they would visit me in hospital. I felt he had let them down badly, a pattern of behaviour that manifest in our marriage, that they were now subjected to in his care, which would only serve to reinforce the confusion and disorientation they would feel at this difficult time. It seemed as though the children's needs were last on his list of priorities, something that was made very clear in the Cassel Report. His focus, while aimed at hurting me, also disregarded the feelings of others as he continued this stormy route of destruction.

Jonathan's obvious desire to see Alice and no doubt persistent pressure from the children to see me, led him to contact Social Services again, and although they were no longer involved, he requested a visit at a 'supervised' centre. One would have assumed their response would have been a no, considering the outcome of our recent Child Protection meeting. As always though, Social Services jumped to his every request. In saying yes, they documented that he based the petition on the need for the children to be safe in the presence their violent mother, admitting he had prevented their hospital visit for this very reason.

Painful though it was to read, I had to wonder if Jonathan was either completely deluded or trying to build a case around 'violence' for the impending court hearing, as so far he had failed to prove any form of mental illness. It appeared both the former and latter were true, as out of the blue he had managed to have this new accusation not only in his files, but in the folders of Social Services too. The agreement was communicated to me and I was informed that I would be allowed to see Harry, Annie and Alfred for one hour 'supervised.' Jonathan at the same time would be allowed to hold Alice, whilst remaining in a separate room.

Like a puppet on a string I dutifully turned up at the designated time and venue. With Alice in her car seat I carried her into a 1970's redbrick, flat roofed, cold and soulless building, which mirrored the severity that Social Services in Twickenham had thus far revealed.

I was greeted at the door of the contact centre and Alice was removed from me in a manner which made me feel I was embarking on a prison sentence, before being escorted into a room where my three beautiful children were waiting. Their squeals of delight and pleasure were as evident as ever when they noticed I had arrived. They ran up to me longing to tell me their many stories. I hugged them and held them remembering how I had done so many times before in circumstances which were less harsh than today. I could not contain my feelings and tears raced down my cheeks at this reunion. In the back of my mind was the knowledge that the children would be taken from me permanently, against both their wishes and mine, and the inevitable parting dominated my mind.

I noticed Harry had found some ride-on vehicles which he moved towards in a small outside area and I carried Alfred to see with what he wished to play.

Annie only had questions to ask. I dried my face and braved the inquisition that flew my way:

> *"Can we come home with you Mummy?"*
> *"Where is Alice Mummy?"*
> *"Do you not want us Mummy?"*
> *"Do you not love us Mummy?"*
> *"Why can't we be with you Mummy?"*

It was heart-wrenching, but no more so than it had been in those early days in November when I was only allowed to see the children on restricted supervised visits. I remembered them being peeled off my legs as they were taken away on each occasion, leaving them screaming ear-piercing cries that still echoed in my head today. As much as I was trying to enjoy seeing them, I could not escape from what I knew was soon to happen. In a moment they would be untwined from me, like a wrapped vine being ripped from its support once more.

There was a woman in the room who watched my every manoeuvre; she shifted whenever I moved, staying within only a few feet of me, going outside as I went outside and returning inside as I did the same. I wondered if she performed this job day in and day out, and what she would make of the bond between the children and I. Would she feel what the police officer felt and know that this was wrong? I doubted it and imagined her to be like all the other officers I had met. I could tell by her bland expression and lack of warmth that she was not an empathetic woman and probably could never understand what my children might be suffering right now. I wondered if she had toddlers or even teenagers of her own, and concluded that most parents coming into this place would simply all have labels hanging over their heads which would read as, 'failed.'

The children played a little, but mostly asked questions insecurely. I guess they knew the inevitable like me, as they must have already been told they would not be coming home. Annie was beside herself pleading and begging and there was nothing I could say that would console her, she needed me and that was that. Nothing other than coming home with me that day would have brought a smile to her face. The boys were focused in determined play, but knowing them so well, I saw their attempt at forced distraction, so as not to face the reality of all that was going on. In many ways they were more able to protect themselves than Annie, who again wore her heart on her sleeve, but at the same time I saw utter brokenness in them all. It was like watching animals who had been beaten so badly giving in so as to not have to fight.

All three children had returned to the haunted internal place they had previously been in. Peace was gone and they manifested behaviour of being deeply disturbed. Anger rose in me at a system that could not only allow this, but be the cause of it all. What lay ahead for these small children who had suffered so much devastation in their short lives and how much more could their spirits be broken? I knew there was love but was there any hope that they would one day fully heal?

Inevitably the hour came to an end, and as though a bell had rung at the end of an exam session I was ushered out of the room with barely a chance to say goodbye. My three small children screamed, cried and shouted as they tried all they could in a vain attempt to make their mother take them home. I was devastated and more hurt was hurled onto the pile already high enough. Raw pain pierced my body as we were separated once again. Alice was returned to my care and I drove away in tears. If I could hardly bear such pain, what would my children be feeling when they had so few resources to call upon? In the eyes of the professionals we had come here today to 'protect' my children but the truth was it would be yet another occasion where they would be emotionally and psychologically destroyed. I could barely allow my mind to imagine them returning to a home that was not theirs, and a place where the comfort they so required would not be found.

CHAPTER NINETEEN

The meeting that had just taken place was another rock-bottom moment for me amid so many lows of the previous months, and it did something grave to lower my spirits even more. Confidence in the system vanished again from the short lived moment at the child protection conference. As we neared another court hearing I expected injustice would be repeated and another ruling would be made in favour of the children's father. Hope had been suspended for so long and I had come to a place of accepting a miscarriage of justice. Helplessness and exhaustion took a gentle toll and became responsible for preventing my fighting spirit from revealing itself, for fear of repeated hurt.

The High Court hearing had already been scheduled. Within days I walked anxiously once more into the intimidating Royal Courts of Justice, curious whether they would indeed live up to their name. I wondered what this awe-inspiring landmark, in the centre of London's Fleet Street would represent to many who appeared inside. To me they personified the heart of suffering of so many people, families in particular, which were being ripped apart by rulings made by judges in an outdated system, which seemed archaic. If parents were being failed as I was, how much more so were the children, who appeared to have no voice? I had recently been reading in the press many cases like mine and I longed to reveal all that was going on and have a story splattered all over a tabloid for the world to read. The reputable charity Mothers Apart from Their Children (MATCH), revealed story after story of the terrible trauma caused by the separation of children from their parents. As I recounted all I had read, I became aware I was standing in one of the buildings that was historically instrumental in narrating the above.

Although the Court of Appeal returned my children by overruling the decision of the judge in Brentford County Court, I placed no trust in the system I was in. It seemed the outcome reflected only the amount of money one was able to pay, and Jonathan seemed able to produce a lot of it.

Alice had just reached the age of two weeks and accompanied me up to London. We were driven by Maria who lovingly escorted us and put her own needs aside at this sad time for her. She was a tower of strength, as was Laura who was by my side again, with Peter encouraging us on. It was one thing to sit through the meeting in Social Services alone, but I would have struggled to do it in court, and I knew the presence of those I loved so dearly would strengthen my resolve to fight. I felt carried by their tremendous love at this time; overwhelmingly denying themselves and their needs as they had borne my pain and grief for so long.

To my surprise and astonishment a female judge entered and we stood to show her respect, taking our places only as she sat. She introduced herself sitting upright in her chair and I recognized some of the same compassion I saw in the psychiatrist in Kingston Hospital. We had to request Alice be allowed to enter the court, because she was still being breastfed, and not only had I no one to leave her with, but it also went against court rules to take her in. The judge agreed on condition that if she cried I would immediately take her out. Alice was as good as gold and lay on my lap sleeping while the barristers introduced the case. Her Ladyship, I noticed, spent some time observing me as they presented the evidence and she listened to each party in turn. I couldn't stop myself from being concerned that someone who had again never met me had the authority to speak on my behalf. At the same time though, I admired my barrister's eloquence and quick thinking, revealing both his intelligence and his ability to act, as though in a play on stage. There was a court language that they all entered into and this time I felt I was watching a game of volleyball in a sports arena staged with seating for the spectators. As the ball passed from player to player, each one looked intent on getting the ball over a net, positioned incredibly high.

The judge paused as the speeches ended and taking off her glasses, rested them unhurriedly on the bench, as she responded. Looking intently at my husband's counsel she asked:

"How did this lady get to hospital when she delivered this child? Was anyone with her when the husband was absent? Without any money, how did she get there?"

I liked her immediately, feeling hugely relieved that this case, which was going to be long, was not being heard by a man. The judge had undoubtedly given birth herself and knew well the basic human requisite at such a time. She appeared able to cut herself off from what the barristers were saying and enquire of my circumstances. I looked behind me to those who had come to support me and saw the pleasure on their faces mirroring mine. I then looked at Jonathan who was almost beside me in the same row and wondered whether he regretted not being at the birth of his fourth child.

Alice remained asleep on my lap and I felt deep gratitude that I had not lost her, as I had feared so many times, as the pressure had taken its toll. I also felt tremendously proud of her tenacity to survive through all the stress my body had endured in the nine month preparation for her entry into the world. She awoke at that moment and I discreetly fed her, hoping no one would notice as she suckled and fell immediately back to sleep.

We broke for lunch and returned for more evidence, much of which had been heard in the previous court case. In addition however, was the new documentation acquired from the psychiatric reports from Kingston Hospital and the Child Protection Conference files, which were submitted at the request of my legal team. The transcript from the ex parte hearing was read by the petitioner's legal representatives. They seemed to hope that the judge's ruling at that time could be evidence in their favour, even though it had since been overturned. I guess they desired to emphasise the urgent necessity to remove not only the three older children from my care, but the baby too. Their argument was; risk from a dangerously ill mother.

In response, like rolling a higher number on the dice, or playing the best card which they had kept aside, my silk threw in the overruling summary and read the judge's own words. He spoke of her disquiet that she had not known the full facts of the case when making her ruling, and stated if she had heard Lord Thornton's thoughts she never would have removed the children. The reversing of her decision was presented along with her reasons. He cleverly highlighted that although at the time the children could not be returned to my care, due to the fact I was still in hospital, I was now back in our house and ready for their homecoming.

Evidence continued late into the early earning, by which time we were reminded that the court was closing and we would have to reappear the following day. Although disappointing, at least the judge's diary was free, or otherwise it could have been a lengthy wait for another scheduled session. We left when the court was dark and were the last to exit the premises. There only remained a few security personnel, who saw us out of the building, before locking it for the night and leaving, possibly glad like us that their day had ended.

I was tired and not surprisingly once more emotionally wiped-out, having not slept that previous night for adrenalin rushing around my body. I was desperate to know the outcome, but not wishing to presume anything, as with any game, winning and losing can switch from side to side so easily, and one can never guess the result until the very last few seconds.

I was up early the next day and driven into London by Maria for the last time. We purchased a quick coffee to calm our nerves at the cafe around the corner from the law courts, where we had visited before. We slipped our bags onto the security conveyor belt, as though passing through an airport terminal, and walked to the same room we had been in the previous day. More evidence was heard and I looked at the piles of files which had been brought into court on trolleys. I remembered my solicitor telling me that their volume monopolised the space in her garage, giving an indication of the quantity of information submitted. The 'Blue' File' still dominated the evidence of the opposition collated on Jonathan's behalf. As I peered at their presence, I heard in my mind Emily's words, *they are clutching at straws because they have nothing on you'.*

The discussion went backwards and forwards; voices became heated as allegations were made and never ending arguments presented. The two legal teams proved everything logically using whatever form they could; intellectualism, eloquence, manipulation, control and also downright arrogance. At times I managed to abandon the emotion of what was being relayed and observe the stage. The participants almost played a war scene, with an impending victory or defeat and I observed carefully the strategies which both sides depended on. It became apparent the 'silks' had calculated knowledge of the strengths and weaknesses of the opponents and were using the most powerful weapons they could to counterattack or invade.

My eyes moved from the warriors to the army general, or rather the judge, who carefully scrutinized every move, declining some as obvious foul play. We adjourned for lunch as the judge confirmed she was satisfied she had heard all the evidence. We would reconvene to hear her summing up.

Judge Margaret Hemp commenced her introduction by highlighting many of the injustices that had already been exposed. She reinforced her distaste for Dr Harwell's unethical diagnosis, which Jonathan's legal team were still using as evidence. She drew attention to the unusual nature of Social Services' involvement, questioning their position when no assessments had been made. She highlighted the determination of the opposition to prove mental illness, regardless of the evidence before them. Then she focused on the most recent hospital psychiatric assessment from Kingston Hospital, which contradicted everything that was said in the Cassel report.

At this point she questioned the role of Dr Kimberly. He was appointed by Lord Thornton at the Court of Appeal hearing in December, yet had not once appeared for any of the assessments at the Cassel. She appreciated the evidence that my legal team had presented which revealed neither of the two psychologists were qualified to diagnose Borderline Personality Disorder, and pointed out that one only held 'play therapist' or her list of credentials. She asked on what grounds Dr Kimberly based his findings, other than Dr Harwell's opinion. She queried why he had signed his name to the report without ever demonstrating why he thought the children should reside with the father. Furthermore she queried the assumption that I suffered from Borderline Personality Disorder, when all other psychiatrists who had actually met me said otherwise.

She deduced from the information at hand that the judge at the ex parte hearing was misguided four weeks earlier. She presupposed Judge Holmes had made an erroneous decision in removing the children from me, attributing her judgment to insufficient and inadequate material in her possession. She said she had absolutely no information before her to suggest any of the children would have been harmed by me, and hence logic suggested there had been no reason whatsoever to remove any of them so abruptly from my care.

She also questioned how she could keep the children from their mother who had demonstrated that she was able to care appropriately for Alice. She pointed out that she had witnessed for herself first hand, the bond and close relationship between mother and child in court. Her description emphasised how I had cared beautifully for Alice over the past two days, something she added, she had never seen whilst sitting in session before. Finally she challenged the rationale behind preventing the children's return, when even Social Services had failed to find a single reason to place Alice on the child protection register. The unanimous decision by the professionals involved verified the unsubstantial need for the organisation to play any role in our lives.

Indignation rose in her voice as she described the catastrophic consequences on the children, who knew their mother had a new baby in their absence and without their involvement. She discussed the probable likelihood of feelings of rejection, and/or of being replaced or displaced, as they were denied seeing their mother. She ruled that Harry, Annie and Alfred be returned immediately home to the care of their mother and the interim residence order to be awarded to me. She ruled also that a court date be set in October, three months later, to decide the final residence order for all four children. In the meantime she requested a psychiatric assessment for 'both' parents by an independent psychiatrist. She also ordered a full Cafcass (children and family court advisory and support service) report detailing observations of the children with their parents individually and in their home setting. She asked too that Dr Kimberly account for his signature on the Cassel report and there be a meeting of expert witnesses with him present.

CHAPTER TWENTY

For the second time the High Court had reinstated the interim residence order to me and hence the children to my care. I was elated and overjoyed to think I was to see my children so very soon. More importantly they could return to my arms and the safe environment where they belonged. The judge had not failed my children, but was astute and had operated from a place of grace, integrity and wisdom. From the beginning I had liked her and now felt privileged that she was at the hearing. It revealed to me that having one's children returned through court is really dependent on the skill, expertise and experience of the legal team employed. The court system appeared in my mind to be flawed because it favoured those with money, but with Legal Aid behind me I was able to be represented by one of the best silks in town. Without that, I believe a judge sitting in session that day might have ruled a very different outcome.

The children were brought home the following morning by their father. Their delivery replicated their last 'drop off', where three little people rushed to the door and knocked vigorously, with such an air of excitement that my heart pounded like a quickened beat of a drum. The three of them rushed into the house and went from room to room, checking that everything they knew as familiar had remained the same. They saw Alice sitting in her little chair, asleep in the dining room and rushed up to see her, overwhelmed that her presence graced their return. The children were excited to be home and the end of our second long separation had come. The joy was indescribable, mingled with feelings of relief and exhaustion. I was thrilled, but realistic that I had to face not only three returned children in trauma, but also a new baby to look after. I had to pick up the pieces from our lives that had been ripped once more to shreds.

I was overjoyed at the children being home and was over the moon as they ran into my arms in disbelief that they were allowed to again return. They were excited to have the chance to sleep in their beds, be reunited with their toys and eat the food they loved. For them familiarity was so important in enabling them to feel stable and secure, so the healing could once more resume. I was aware that they had descended into deeper distress than they had previously been in; something which seemed hard to believe. This time not only had they been taken away, but it was nullifying all the promises I had made; that a similar thing could never happen again. It was going to be difficult to present the same reassurance to them all. We had so many obstacles to get through, namely the invasion of our privacy by Cafcass. If this agency were anything like Social Services, I still had a battle on my hands.

How Jonathan would respond to his recent loss could never be presumed. I knew he was not going to back off before the final residence order was decided, even though he should have been advised to do so. What he had been capable of orchestrating I had never suspected before it occurred, but his machinations had become publicly evident. How much further he would go was still to be seen. I didn't doubt for one minute that he had more cards to play and I worried as to how many surplus he had hidden up his sleeve.

The court order stipulated the children stay with their father every other weekend, which unsettled them. He also had designated times for seeing Alice, which without doubt was always when she was in need of a feed. I would hand her over through a mutual friend and seeing as there was no regular nursing pattern at only two weeks old, she would invariably be taken off me mid-feed and screaming as she went. I was sure even at this young age she sensed the animosity and knew she should not have been passed over in this manner from her mother's breast. Jonathan deviated however, not one minute from the time that was earmarked in his allocated sessions. Painfully, I would hear Alice's cry as he took her away from our friend's house and she would often return red faced and puffy an hour later, still screaming and distressed. This was a man who wanted evidence to prove I was pregnant, wanted her taken off me at birth and placed into care. I felt so very sad.

My thoughts knotted into confusion each time I handed her over. I could not understand his insistence to see her. Fear of her abduction dominated my every thought and although it never actually materialised, I never felt peace in handing her over. Furthermore I remained concerned about the lengths to which he would go to make us all miserable.

For obvious reasons this was a decidedly unsettled time for the children and I. Family and friends gathered around to provide the support we needed. As they delighted at the news of their second return, they were happy to help in any way they could. In fact it appeared as if nothing was too much for them, as they all rallied around. So many people were pleased at the children's homecoming the house became filled with cards and flowers, gifts and food. We celebrated this victory, as the phone never stopped ringing and a constant stream of visitors came to our door. Friends I knew well, as well as other acquaintances became suddenly suspicious of all Jonathan was doing, vindicating me from the allegations he had made. Others, who had previously ignored me, suddenly began to speak, inviting me to their homes and showing a genuine interest in what was going on. Those who had remained away came and knocked on my door expressing genuine pleasure that the children were home.

Our local church organised a roster to provide us all with three meals a day and food, not dissimilar from what one could find at Fortnum and Mason, began arriving at our Victorian home, cooked by our friends. Spaghetti bolognese, roast meals, pies, stews, soups, casseroles and dishes of all different nationalities graced our table. They were accompanied by desserts of every kind; homemade cakes, biscuits, chocolates, soft drinks and wine. As more and more kept arriving my freezer became full to the brim. This meal provision was occasionally accompanied by a supermarket internet shop which would arrive on my doorstep. For more than a three month period I didn't have to either shop or cook. I later discovered there had been a waiting list for people to add their names to the roster, such was the generosity of those around.

The children and I received gifts of every kind and newly donated toys excited them. Money appeared through our letterbox from unknown donors, which meant I could pay the bills that sat in a pile by my door. I had never before been in a place to receive such extraordinary generosity and right now I wasn't going to say no, as we had no income of our own. Being relieved of the shopping let alone the cooking was a welcome reprieve to the otherwise exhausting circumstances I found myself in. It was a humbling time. The experience was beginning to teach me to gracefully accept the provision being offered by so many people who just wanted to help. It wasn't an easy thing for someone who was highly capable and who had previously been fiercely independent, but I obviously had lessons to learn.

The goodwill continued through the summer holidays as another family offered us their three bedroom beach house in Margate. It meant we could all get out of London, visit the coast and have a welcome break. They knew we would otherwise not get away so gave us their beautiful little 1940's period cottage by the sea, lavishing on us eiderdowns instead of duvets and wall paper that matched the curtains. The garden lined with lavender, was filled with flowers and the lawn was dotted with trees bearing fruit. Of course, to make the setting complete a swing hung at the perfect height for the little ones to play. Their kindness was such that they also employed a charming nanny for us, who they hired for the week. She appeared like Mary Poppins to help me look after four children who enjoyed this girl's youthfulness, energy and sense of fun.

It was a dream come true as my elderly father joined us and stayed in a hotel nearby. My sister and her children visited from Berkshire and we shared some truly memorable moments. We played on the beach, dug sandcastles, swam in the sea and simply enjoyed some re-bonding time as a family. The summer break was exactly what was needed to regroup and assess the level of damage that required repairing, as we knew that before any of that could begin we just needed to 'be'.

Each of the children demanded constant reassurance that they didn't have to go and live with their grandparents again. They told of how difficult the circumstances were; where there was no patience for noise or seemingly even a change of routine. Affection was limited as they were not a family open to cuddles, so the environment was quite alien from the home they knew.

The psychological impact on the children of their second removal was immense. Harry having been convinced I had died on his first taking, continued to repeat it when he returned home on this occasion. All three were bed wetting and had developed unhealthy eating habits. They had recurring nightmares of being driven away by police cars, disappearing on houses floating away on boats down rivers and being taken by strangers in the streets. They were insecure and jumpy, never knowing if they would be snatched again. Lacking in confidence, their concentration and development was affected, so also was their ability to connect with friends and interact socially with others around.

Annie in particular verbalised all that had gone on. She angrily described her fear that she would never come home and the dread that she would never see me again. She was jumpy and nervous when there was a knock on the door and ran and hid under a table or chair if someone came in. This was behaviour which continued for many years to come and would later require professional help to treat. She could no longer walk down the street without clutching my side; for fear that anyone would steal her away. She began having panic attacks if she was separated from me for any length of time, also needing to hold me all night in order to remain asleep. She was the most sensitive and emotional of all four and nothing could remain hidden even if she tried. She talked and talked, which I read as a good sign, glad for opportunity that her fears could be expressed. She had been such a happy, strong, independent child, one who would skip down the road with not a care in the world, other than picking the flowers that leant over the neighbour's walls. Now however she looked gaunt and pale, carrying the weight of the universe on her shoulders, withdrawing into a distant world where her true self could not be reached.

Alfred was angry in a way he had never been before. If I thought he was traumatised on his last return I was in for a shock now. His speech stopped developing and he remained silent, not talking for a further eighteen months following his latest return. He needed to be carried everywhere, crying if I left his sight or even entered another room, whining constantly with a pain that came from deep within. The sounds were ones I had not heard before and were like that of a whimpering animal that had been beaten. Emotionally he had been crushed again and again at an age where he could not yet verbalise his needs, let alone understand why on earth he deserved all he had endured. As he stopped speaking he communicated only through his eyes, his tears and his cries. There was nothing I could do other than hold him and be there to reassure him and love him, hoping one day he would find joy again in his bleak internal world.

Harry was brave, so very brave, and entered into an imaginary world where he could escape from the pain rather than face it, as it was all too raw. He knew, like me, it would rip him apart like a lion with its prey and he needed to just survive each day. Disappearing into his own internal mind was the only way he knew and I admired him as we all struggled to find ways to get through, one moment at a time.

Some days felt like we were all drowning and the life jackets we needed seemed too far away to reach. We splashed around and did the best we could to stay afloat holding onto each other for as long as we were able. Alice was as good as gold and brought much joy to us all. She smiled and started to make expressions at her siblings in return for their humourous entertainment. Little blessings and small pleasures would get us through each day, as we took one step at a time through the weeks ahead, tended our fragile wounds, held one another and survived.

CHAPTER TWENTY-ONE

It was the beginning of September and no sooner had we arrived back from our holiday on the Kent coast, there was a knock on the door from our newly appointed Cafcass officer. She had been immediately assigned to our case. She was eager to get under way and start her assessments, describing how time was short until the October hearing. I excused the yet unpacked cases from our time away and introduced her to the children. As I brought the remaining items out of the car, I dumped the buckets and spades fresh with sand on our wooden floor in the hallway, and the piles of washing by the laundry room door.

We had already spoken on the phone and she had explained that Cafcass assess over 145,000 children and young people a year going through care or adoption proceedings. She clarified that she would be the voice of my children in the family court. Her role was to supposedly ensure that their welfare was put first during the court dispute, where my husband and I were unable to agree about future arrangements for them all.

Today she had come to meet us and introduce the format of what would lie ahead. She initiated contact with the children by interviewing them one by one upstairs in Annie's bedroom, out of earshot so I could not hear what was being said. It was ironic that we teach our children to not talk to strangers and yet here, was a system that was forcing mine to do just that. They had to speak to someone they had never met, without their mother present and express their innermost feelings when they were so traumatised they could barely say hello. As I expected they were not forthcoming and nor should they have been. The absence of speech however, did not deter her from making other observations and she seemed impressed by the peaceful atmosphere in the home and the range of things they could do. We ate tea and showed the officer all she wanted to see, from the layout of the bedrooms, to the kitchen and bathroom facilities, the garden with the sandpit and tree house. She asked to see the toys the children engaged with and spent some time trying to encourage Harry who was playing with a mountain of his cuddly animals, sensing they were on his 'important' list in life.

In making an initial judgment—which through necessity I had become accustomed to doing—I decided the officer was probably going to record some unity and calm in our home if nothing else. I decided that maybe I didn't have to write her off immediately, but give her a chance, as she spent more time with us over the next few coming days. Already she had ticked a few positive boxes in my mind, as I registered that I thought she was patient, a good listener, organised and fairly kind. So far she beat hands down anyone I had ever met in Twickenham Social Services. Also to my surprise, I noticed how she had actually asked me questions and inquired how I felt. She was receptive to hearing my opinion about the circumstances I had found myself in, was interested in what was going on and appeared to be genuine in her considerate approach to interviewing us all.

Following this initial appointment, the Cafcass officer returned for several visits and on each occasion she got to further identify the children's individual personalities. As they felt safer with her and trusted she wasn't going to take them away, they opened up more and more of all they wished to say. They revealed a little of their idiosyncrasies, character traits, interests, fears and desires. Individually, they in turn talked of their love of being at home, and volunteered information about the things we did together, what we ate, where we went, who our friends were and the fun we had. I was so proud of them talking of their pain and how hard it had been to stay away. They quite openly brought me into all of their conversations, as though we belonged together and I sensed the unity we shared.

During her visits there were always knocks on the door from friends and neighbours, who would appear at our house two or three times a day. They would arrive with something to drop off, or with a snippet from the newspaper, or with a gift for the children, or simply pop by for a chat. Friends from the baby groups I had been in and mums from the school, all lived only a few streets away and would often call in, as well as cousins who were still dropping off gifts or cards for little Alice.

By this stage the Cafcass officer was beginning to open up a little and started to express enough thoughts to enable me to read some of her impressions. She commented on how many people we appeared to know and what a lively and supportive neighbourhood it seemed. I appreciated her remarks, guessing she needed to see that we had support around. I wondered if she had read in the 'Blue File' how I had no friends and how the ones that I did have all thought I was mentally ill. At least if she saw evidence first hand that was contrary to what she read about me, she might begin to get the picture. On one of her visits she had planned to come at a time that clashed with Harry and Annie's school pick up in early September. It was the perfect opportunity to walk her through the village of St Margaret's, as she had mentioned that she would like to see the area in which we lived.

St Margaret's is a quiet gentrified village in outer London tucked neatly between Richmond and Twickenham. It follows the loop of the River Thames, with Marble Park sitting comfortably in the bend of the river. In the midst of the grounds sits Marble Hill House, a beautiful Palladian villa positioned in the sixty six acres of attractive riverside parkland. The dwelling was built for Henrietta Howard, mistress of King George II, when he was Prince of Wales and friend and confidante of some of the cleverest men in England. The house recalls perfectly the atmosphere of fashionable Georgian life, as does the row of Georgian buildings beside the park, which is one of the area's most desirable streets in which to live.

A ferry by the water's edge takes passengers across the river to Petersham Meadows, where cows have been grazing since the latter years of the 19th century. It neighbours Ham House, presently in the hands of The National Trust, standing as one of Europe's greatest 17th Century houses. Many young families choose to move into the area due to the reputation of the four schools and because of the amount of open space available. With opportunities for young children to walk and play, it has also become known for being family friendly and safe.

The children always loved walking through Richmond Park amused at the deer, which stopped the traffic as they ran across the road. We loved cycling on our bicycles along the water's edge, taking boat rides up the river, having picnics on Richmond green and enjoying the fairs on Moor Mead Park. We would only need to step out of our front door to enjoy the eclectic and lively street fairs organised by the association of shopkeepers, who donated the proceeds to the four local schools.

Lost in memories of all we had previously done as a family, I put Alfred and Alice into the double buggy. The officer and I dropped into a couple of shops before going to the school together to collect the two older children. We discussed our allotment on the way, which we had been working on for the past two years and I explained the attraction of a mini community of keen, healthy food growers where the local children could meet.

The first shop we entered was a second hand children's clothes shop which I often frequented and knew the owner well. She was enchanted with meeting Alice for the first time, saying how excited she had been, and of course commented on the dramas of the past few weeks. She told me she and so many others were absolutely thrilled to hear the children were home and that we were together, reunited as a family again once more. The second shop was the health food shop where again I knew the proprietor well. Some similar, appropriately timed comments were made, within full earshot of the officer who remained by my side. We bumped into several groups of friends leaving the store, as the well-known and very popular cafe owner next door called out to say hello. The gallery owner, a good friend of mine who had hung some of my paintings over the years popped out as we passed, with a lolly for Alfred who was patiently absorbing all that was going on.

We continued walking to the infant school and chatted to mums, taking in the usual buzzing atmosphere while we walked through the secure front gates. An organised array of modernised, Victorian buildings lay before us, where the children spent their days. The classrooms were centred around open, communal spaces, with climbing frames, children's play areas and a wonderful nature garden which all of mine adored. It was where Harry had excitedly contributed to the art on the outside wall, by creating a butterfly, as part of a class mural scene.

As eventually the classroom doors opened signalling the end of the school day, we collected Annie and Harry who greeted us with squeals of excitement, as they ran into my arms to be hugged. The infant school enrolled children from 'rising threes' in the nursery department, to seven year olds in the year two class and prepared the village children for the junior school only a few streets away. It had been extremely important in our lives and symbolised such security for the children, simply through the routine of walking there, two or three times a day and being greeted by those we knew. The teachers were influential stabilising figures for the children, as they knew what had been going on and were hugely supportive, offering to do anything they could for us all. Minnie the dinner lady had been there over twenty five years, and soon to be retiring, adored Harry. It naturally meant the world to him during his time there in the day, as he regarded her as a nurturing grandmother who simply loved his company. She kept a special watch out for both of the children at break times in the playground, making sure they were never alone and encouraging them each day, reporting back to me any progress they made.

I was aware that the officer was not only watching my every move but listening to each conversation, and I started to see from her perspective what she might be looking out for, to write in her report. A smile came across my face as I looked on our lives here with new eyes, to things I had before taken so much for granted. I had never appreciated so much the gift of living in such a beautiful area, nor the love shown by so many friends, the facilities we used so often and the roots which we had put down during the last few years. Not only had my children returned home, but I realised we were in a position where we were held safe by everything around us, as we continued to lick our wounds.

CHAPTER TWENTY-TWO

The next session with the Cafcass officer was a one on one, with me and her alone. We met in a room somewhere in Kingston, in an office that smelt of the same rotten carpets and cigarette smoke as Brentford County Court. No sooner was I in there, than I ached to get out. We sat on two chairs awkwardly, one opposite the other, and she filled in notes on her pad, as she questioned me for what seemed like an eternity. She asked about my life, my career, my family and my relationship with Jonathan. Her first question probed into my marriage and I answered truthfully identifying the struggle mainly with usual stresses of balancing shifting needs, changing careers and the well-known demands of raising a young family. I described how I had experienced four pregnancies in only a couple more years.

We had married in 1997, had our first child in 1998, second in 2000, third in 2002, and I was pregnant with our 4th on the last day of our married life together in 2003. I had given up an exciting career as Head of Art at the United World College in Singapore. It was one of the largest schools in the world and certainly the top at the time offering the International Baccalaureate; the highly acclaimed international examination system. I was examining for the IB and involved in training programmes for the visual arts, teaching a subject I loved and immersed in a culture that reflected an international mix of the exotic.

I had been a lightweight rower and successfully competed to a respectable level. I had travelled the world and taught in boarding schools in England, Asia and Australia, as well as lived on a kibbutz in Israel. I thoroughly enjoyed life to the full being outgoing, loving adventure and having a great social life wherever I lived. I admitted however, I could not claim credit for being the perfect wife. I had gone from being independent, sociable, happy and successful, to feeling isolated, worthless, frustrated and withdrawn.

Having met Jonathan many times during the 1980's, we re-established contact at a friend's wedding in 1996 in London. I had just been offered a job in Singapore and it was he that followed me there. Within four months of starting a relationship we moved together to start a new life in the Far East and I began work.

We lived in an isolated bubble away from my in-laws, whom I barely knew, and on our own we created what I perceived to be quite a selfish life as we chose. We had plenty of money and could afford to live in a beautiful condominium with our own swimming pool and tennis court. We ate out, bought whatever we wanted, holidayed, travelled and spent many weekends lazing on sunny decks on the water's edge in a range of alluring Asian resorts. One minute we were in Indonesia, the next Malaysia, then Borneo, Vietnam, Thailand and Bali.

I was participating on, and leading adventure trips with students mountain biking and trekking on local islands. We took children to

Mt Kinabalu, climbing the highest mountain in South East Asia. We kayaked through rainforests, white water rafted through rivers in the jungle, hiked through plantations and went on Outward Bound trips to our education centre in Tama Nagara, Malaysia. When Harry was born we employed our own amah to cook for us, clean, wash, shop and basically pamper to our every need. I returned to work unwillingly as I had wanted to remain at home with my first baby, but life was easy and to be perfectly honest we could have wanted for nothing more.

After only three years in Singapore however, Jonathan was bored with his working life. He had found a prestigious job on the north of the island, in a flourishing shipyard managing a large building project, but wanted to resume his career in London. He needed to be less isolated and back in the market 'where it was all happening', but I didn't want to go. I did not want to leave Singapore, the life we had built and the friends we had made, nor did I want to give up my job which I loved. I was nervous and remembered his words back in 1996:

"It will be good for me to leave the drinking culture in London and start afresh."

Alarm bells rang and I was reluctant to leave Asia for London. I mentioned to the officer the fear I had for our marriage should Jonathan be more influenced by a city culture fuelled by alcohol and I was worried about what lay ahead.

I described to the Cafcass officer what occurred when I was due to deliver our first baby in Singapore. Jonathan would come home each day begging me not go into labour, telling me he had consumed too much alcohol, but that 'tomorrow' he would stop drinking. When eventually labour did start he disappeared off to the cricket club, as I sat alone through a painful, arduous day alone.

Each hour he would phone to say he would, 'only have one more'. I felt lousy and inadequate when I eventually had to call him away. Immediately on arrival at hospital he fell asleep on the bed beside me, snoring as I called for help.

Harry's birth was long and complicated. He was back to front and instead of recommending a caesarean, the obstetrician put her foot on the bed as she tried to pull him out with forceps. It took five eventual attempts which left me with a cracked pelvis and haemorrhaging, complicated by a rapidly rising fever. Left too weak to move, let alone able to pick up Harry and feed him, I needed Jonathan to be present and support me both mentally and physically. It was at that moment however, that he left to meet a friend for a drink and 'wet the baby's head', and abdicating responsibility for his child and me, he disappeared.

Whilst Harry had been left physically scarred from the difficult forceps delivery, the procedure left me needing urgent medical attention. I described to the officer, how I felt alone in a foreign country with no parents or anyone that I knew that had children to help look after the baby. Needing re-admission into hospital, I struggled to lift Harry in his heavy car seat, and felt remorse that my husband could not support me or be by my side. I made my way back into the obstetrics ward, having to take Harry with me into theatre, while as I was operated on under local anaesthetic. My return journey home was made to an empty house, where there was no food, but plenty of bills left to pay and I remained bed bound while Jonathan took not a single day off work.

By the time I was pregnant with our second child, we were back in England and I had given up my job which I loved. I found London claustrophobic, the weather depressing, the houses tiny and the general attitude one of depression. Our life was no longer outside in the sunshine, but stuck indoors in the grey, and in the rain and the cold. We bought ourselves a small Victorian house which burdened us financially, and on one salary we could no longer afford to eat out, or pay for the pleasures we had been selfishly indulging in. Travelling and holidays ended abruptly along with all the fun in our relationship as I became lost in sadness at our return. I felt I mattered little in our marriage, and the lack of conversation about our return did little to lift my morale.

Not surprisingly, Jonathan began to stay out late, meeting work colleagues in the evenings and building up his new life in the city. He travelled regularly on long overseas trips, and the company he worked for encouraged the use of alcohol as the norm. Hotel parties, nights away and socialising with clients were expected. I described how he would often have a business lunch which involved heavy drinking, moving from the evening and into the early hours of the morning. It did not help that 'wives' were frowned upon by the owner of the company and 'babies' were the least of what was either convenient or approved of. Although married, Jonathan's boss was not a family man and made it known on several occasions that my husband should put the company before me. I was even ushered out of the only corporate dinner that Jonathan thought I had been invited to, such was the extent of the hostility.

The further time elapsed the more I began to eat alone, parent alone, take the family responsibilities alone and I felt isolated. I missed my mother more than ever, as well as the home she ran. In essence I had nowhere to retreat, to recuperate from the negative impact that drink played on our young family; failed commitments, broken promises and never knowing minute by minute where my husband might be. I had my family around but I needed a home where I could take the children and stay, and my father, as amazing though he was, could not have had us all.

Being a sociable person I built myself a group of friends whom I began to enjoy, but I felt empty and often retreated into isolation. I could not discuss the loneliness within my marriage or my sense of hopelessness at watching my husband disappear into another life which excluded me. I felt I could not betray my marriage and admit to friends who thought we were happily married that I was utterly miserable. Nor could I reveal I was feeling worthless, lost and so very alone. I was living a life which was a lie.

Thursday nights were the big city nights out and by the time the weekend arrived Jonathan was exhausted. As alcohol was a depressive, his personality began to change, as did his motivation, his energy for life and ability to do anything around the home, either with me or our children. I reacted negatively, becoming resentful of broken promises, wasted opportunities and a life which was devoid of fun.

By the time I was pregnant with our third child alcohol had become the third person in our marriage and I felt abandoned to it. Often evenings would begin with a phone call from Jonathan around six o'clock saying:

"I am coming home early. Please don't bath the children, wait until I come home, I would love to bath them myself and will leave now and be home around seven."

Seven would come and go; the children would be tired and restless. I would wait and call Jonathan to find his phone would be switched off, which always meant he had gravitated to a pub or a club, and was not to return home. Sometimes accidentally he would leave it switched on and all I could hear was the background noise in the bar, over him trying to say he had been delayed at work and was still in the office. By eight o'clock I would put the children to bed upset, as they had looked forward to seeing their father. By ten or eleven I would give the last breastfeed to the baby. I would then be woken around two or three by the sound of a taxi drawing up, a pause while he was paid, the slam of the car door and the key in our front porch. On a good night Jonathan could make his way upstairs, but if not I would find him lying on the wooden hall floor already asleep and unable to move. On a bad night he would wake the children and as he fell into his drunken sleep, I was left to breastfeed again a crying baby, exhausted myself and too anxious to rest.

The pattern of behaviour that followed would be dismissal the following day and always a bunch of flowers, to remind me how much he loved me. I didn't know much about the actions of a heavy drinker as I had not experienced this in my own family. Neither could I work out how to respond. Often I was angry; but mainly confused, frustrated, feeling guilty for perhaps imagining he was consuming so much alcohol. I didn't recognise the hurt, the fear, the guilt, nor the anger, turmoil or turbulence. I didn't identify my own blaming attitude or my resentment towards his boss, whom it seemed Jonathan idealised more than me. I was bewildered by arrangements frequently being upset, cancelled or delayed and conversations about those plans being denied. I knew I was isolated and I felt even lonelier as I watched as everyone else's husbands appear home when they said they would, and not break the promises they had made.

By now my self-esteem was at an all-time low and I convinced myself the problem was mine. This in turn would serve to make me try harder, to create a better home, or resolve to communicate what I was feeling, but Jonathan didn't want to know. Remorse for my impatience would then convict me to attempt to become a better wife. I would hide or deny my hurt. Frequently I would plan to cook Jonathan candlelit meals, on evenings when he would be home before ten. Promises of an early return however, always ended up with the switched off phone and me dining alone. I would blow out the candles and put his meal in the fridge for my lunch the following day.

In my mind I went over and over our history and thoughts took me back to our expat days, where I had convinced myself that all was well, but wasn't. I was extremely capable as a person, but felt the weight of responsibility of everything lay on me, even in those early days of our marriage. What I had not understood at that time was the conflict I was juggling with in my mind and how confusing it could be. I came to question whether I was self-obsessed or just narrow-minded, that I felt so very alone, isolated and disconnected. I described to the officer how I felt guilty for wanting my husband by my side, so that we could 'do life together'. In hindsight his absence at a time I was so seriously ill after Harry's birth became the training ground for simply having to cope.

CHAPTER TWENTY-THREE

The Cafcass officer had finally completed her investigations. She probably too was nearing the end of her enquiries with Jonathan and the children, when they stayed the weekends wherever he was now living.

One more assessment had to be made before the return to court and it was one I felt surprisingly peaceful about. This report was court ordered and was to take place with a Dr Somerville, who was a consultant adult psychiatrist working at the Henderson Hospital in Croyden. My remarkably diligent solicitor Emily, had relentlessly spent time researching the criteria required for making a diagnosis of BPD. She was resolute that the consultant should not only be independent, but should come highly esteemed; both of which had not previously been the case. She wanted a recommendation for someone reliable, who had integrity as well as a good reputation, also wishing to prevent Jonathan's legal team coming forward with any proposal we could not trust. In making her inquiries she managed to ascertain, that not only did Dr Somerville hold the qualification necessary for making a diagnosis, but confirmed he actually specialised in the disorder.

Dr Somerville called in mid August to make an appointment, insisting he visit me at home, to save me having to transport a young baby across London. We arranged a mutually convenient date and reassuringly I perceived compassion and empathy in his voice on the end of the phone line, which instantly made me feel safe.

Only a few days later there was a knock on the door at the appointed time and I invited a well dressed, middle aged gentleman into the living room, where I had just started feeding Alice. He insisted on waiting until I had finished, before initiating a conversation so as not to interrupt the feed. He then introduced himself in a kind manner, his intonation being amiable and pleasant to the ear. Speaking softly he began by explaining his background in the field of psychiatry; telling me about the work he undertook, and explaining the qualifications he held. I instantly noticed a subtle receptiveness in him that had never displayed in Social Services, highlighting the dismal lack of appropriate staff that Twickenham employed at that time.

His list of questions was not dissimilar to those I had been asked so many times before and two thoughts crossed my mind. Firstly I wondered how many more interviews I would have sit through whilst repeating my painful story, which was exhausting in itself. Secondly, I thought back to my most recent assessment and was reluctant to get into a rhythm of reciting the tedious answers off by heart, or look as though I could identify the criteria. During the latter months I had been searching information on the internet regarding various different mental health disorders and didn't want to appear too knowledgeable about an area of psychology I should know nothing about.

Dr Somerville reminded me of the Kingston Hospital psychiatrist, displaying the same tentative and unpretentious traits I had appreciated previously. His facial expressions responded to both the distress of the experience that I relayed, as well as the positive moments that had kept me going. Presenting himself professionally, he obviously did not comment on what he was being told, but being a sound reader of facial expressions I perceived both concern and empathy as I continued to speak. My response to his questions came out almost as a monologue in a play, and because I had expressed them so many times before, they almost sounded as though they were rehearsed. Still, the emotion attached to the events never departed and I felt deep wells of sorrow rise, as I recounted the events of the past eleven months, which proved I was still so very raw.

The circumstances had been demanding and wearisome, and I expressed concern to Dr Somerville about the long term emotional harm that would manifest in the children. I described how my own physical body was displaying signs of trauma, as each time I recounted the trials my whole body ached with a pain soon to be identified as chronic fatigue syndrome. It was a debilitating and crippling discomfort that gripped with no relief for twenty four hours a day. My stomach was further affected by the strain I had been under, and coeliac disease was not far from being diagnosed. Although I was happy to discuss the consequence of the tragedies that had occurred, I was careful also to be positive when discussing my emotions and mental health state. I was particularly discerning in what I said and emphasised the support I had around. I knew anything mentioned would be held on record and certainly I wanted nothing that could be used as evidence against me.

The court case had become long and drawn out and I expressed my concern to Dr Somerville that no one in the justice system had yet questioned the mental state of my husband, or queried his motives. He was still conveying to the court through various correspondence, of his deep love for me and his desire for us to be together as a family after I had received the psychiatric care that he suggested. Yet his actions didn't seem like the normal behaviour of a loving husband to me, nor did they seem rooted in compassion. Perturbed that I could not present my own narrative in court, I explained how my solicitor reminded me this case was about proving my innocence, not proving the guilt of another. I expressed my sense of unfairness towards the injustices that flawed the family court.

To reveal the lengths that Jonathan had gone to find evidence against me, I disclosed to Dr Somerville how he had been to court to request access to my GP records dating back to birth. Although reluctant at first because of the medical confidentiality act, the judge agreed, as Jonathan persuaded the court that nothing should remain hidden. I objected because I felt my privacy was being further violated and it seemed nothing in my life could remain out of the public eye. Even my solicitor was shocked and I mentioned her view that Jonathan's obsessive hunt for evidence required her to work to a forensic level to counter all that this man was prepared to attempt. Something she expressed she had never previously done before.

I was devastated and overwhelmed that the judge agreed to my doctor's notes being passed into his hands. It was little consolation that the order stated he could only read them in his solicitor's office, because he wrote extensive notes there. Jonathan was a man who would not deviate from his course and within days he had graphed and documented information from my file, to use against me in court. This new data correlated the number of times I had seen my doctor for recurrent sickness and it enmeshed and intertwined statistics that were being bent to prove a rule.

I guessed he would probably now suggest 'Munchausen Syndrome', as it was something that he had not yet proposed. I was suspicious too because I had read about Dr Harwell on the internet and knew it was something he specialised in, suspecting in

Jonathan's world my recurrent symptoms of coeliac disease would mean so much more. Munchausen Syndrome is a mental illness in which a person repeatedly acts if she or he has a health disorder, when in truth they have caused or imagined the symptoms in order to get special attention or sympathy. What worried me was that having researched Dr Harwell I knew the physical symptoms mirrored mine e.g. chest pain, stomach disorders and so on. I expected this would be the evidence that Jonathan needed to back up his own verdict of mental illness, as he was still collating new information to highlight his case.

As my mind drifted in and out of various developments, Dr Somerville appropriately continued his assessment. Now touching upon an area in my life which took me away from the disappointments, I drifted into more pleasant pastures that were a welcome place to visit.

Information relating to my childhood was obviously of huge consequence in this examination. It could reveal abuse, deprivation or situations that could possibly trigger the need to self-harm. Furthermore it could disclose generational issues that would give a perspective of where I was at today. I passionately described my infant and junior life, with a stay-at-home mum, who immersed herself fully into motherhood and all that came with it. Our days had been filled with picnics, excursions to the beach, and buckets of sand on a rug on the lawn, in our home at the bottom of the North Downs in Kent. We spent our childhood watching our father dig over his vegetable patch and picking frozen sprouts in winter, laden with snow. Both of our parents were keen gardeners and we admired the herbaceous borders blossom through the seasons, the bees pollinate the flowers and the roses display their splendour. The lawn also boasted as its printed, patterned lines reflecting my father's passion. He insisted on mowing each strip three times, so to be in perfect alignment with the lawns on Gardener's Question Time, we viewed on television on a Friday night.

From the age of four we all attended the Convent at the end of the road in Maidstone, where my parents had moved, for the sake of our schooling. We were raised as Catholics and brought up by the nuns who seemed to love our family and taught us well. I was a mischievous child and related to Dr Somerville some of the tricks I played on these seemingly strange ladies, who clothed themselves in black habits. At that age we all desired to know not only what they wore under their long flowing robes, but whether they ever broke from prayer to sleep at night. As lovely though they were, they still seemed strange to a small child and my inquisitive mind would not settle for anything less than discovering the truth for myself. This however was balanced by a healthy appreciation of the opportunity this memorable school offered.

The convent grounds were as tranquil as our gardens at home, with walkways and rose arbours and little wooden shelters where we could hide. I recounted how my soul at this young age was filled with knowledge of the goodness of the land. There was a peace and serenity that fed through to me from all that was around and remained a core part of my being today.

I recaptured how we spent our weekends and holidays with both my parents' siblings. My Irish father was one of seven, and my mother, who had Belgium roots, was a twin in the middle of four. Both sides of the family added profitably to the ever increasing size of the population, with our Uncle Jack having eight, but the average tended to balance around the four mark; our own family obviously bringing into disrepute the tradition of excessive breeding within the Catholic church.

Christmas saw the gathering of cousins on my mother's side with parties on Boxing Day, to eat left over food and we would perform nativity plays, reminding us of what we were celebrating at this exciting time of year. Traditionally they would take place in the hallway or under the staircase in my uncle's beautiful old coach house, lying in the foothills of the North Downs, with far fetching views over the valley below. As children we adored spending time in the extended dormitory style addition, built on primitively for his boys and in the play room tucked neatly under the house. Having no brothers of our own, we were enthusiastic to participate in a lively, if not slightly chaotic household where we were welcomed with open arms and knew we were loved.

I recounted how our holidays would involve family swaps, where we would spend time staying with different aunts and uncles, swim in cousins' pools, play tennis on their courts and ride on their horses. At other times we would play in their boarded attics or playrooms, climb trees, help cook and live as though we belonged. Spending time with our cousins was as much a part of our lives as living with our siblings and something I had very much taken for granted at the time. Now we were all older we made less effort at contacting one another, I guessed because lives were busy, but if there ever was still a family get together, the bond still held strong.

Our own family holidays were on the Kent coast, where we would take a beach house each July. Year after year we would revisit the same places, instilling wonderful memories of a fantasy-like childhood that never passed away. I described to Dr Somerville Dymchurch House; a doctor's holiday residence by the sea which my parents took each summer in our early years. It had a long driveway that led from the beach up to the beautifully proportioned Victorian rambling house, which seemed much bigger than it probably was. I got lost in memories as I described reaching up to open the gate to allow our father's old car to take our luggage down the driveway, its closure essential to keep out the cows from the neighbouring farm. I recalled how we would walk each morning to the farmer's field where we could collect milk from the churns and I talked of the long grass full of summer seed, being taller than we were at the time.

My teen years were interrupted sorrowfully by the closure of the convent. This opened the door to a happy two year period in a 'secondary modern' school where I developed a good network of friends. My skills thrived in in the creative art departments, where I learnt to cook, sew and paint, and my wood and metalwork enthusiasm led me to top grades in the year. My academic results meant I entered the Girls' Grammar at the age of thirteen. Foolishly I chose a more traditional and formal school to the Girls' Technical College which would perhaps have seen me better days, as the attitude of both the head and her deputy at the Grammar during the 80's was not conducive to the education I needed. Both stern and oppressive they dismally cultivated a sombre environment where not many girls thrived. Being slightly rebellious I slipped out of school whenever I wished and opted in for the classes where I knew the teachers were fun.

After narrating several stories to Dr Somerville from my time in education, he moved on to ask me about the passing of my mother and how it had affected my life. He heard how she developed cancer in my teens and how I felt bereft and alone during her extended period of suffering, in hospitals, at home and in nursing centres, where little support was offered. I was truthful in acknowledging that her death was the most traumatic event of my young life and held no restraint in relaying the loss I encountered, not just of her, but in the home she ran.

There was so much more I could say as I chatted from the place I had disappeared into, within my 'inner me'. I realised how much the loss of my mother had been balanced by the beauty, peace, fun and joy which had filled my soul as a very young child. I understood too how she had been responsible for rooting me in a world where love was never doubted and security and stability were not lacking. Sadness came over me as I switched back to the turbulence of the world my children had been exposed to, as I had only ever imagined I would replicate for them all I had enjoyed as a small child.

My mind then suddenly switched away from my younger years

and I came back to sitting on the couch at number three Kings Road with a bang. Feeling as though I had travelled both in time and space in Doctor Who's Tardis, the sudden realisation of why we were here gently filled my eyes with tears.

Dr Somerville filled seemingly endless pages on his pad with his silver ink pen and left thanking me for all I had shared. I was back in Alice's next feed and noticed that three hours had passed on the clock, as I had drifted into such different chapters in my life and recounted them as best I could. I sat and wondered what this next unknown phase would bring. I hoped as much as I could, that it would be an end to all the strife and bring a period of rebuilding from the low place we were all in.

CHAPTER TWENTY-FOUR

It was now late September and copies of evidence for the court continued to arrive in swollen A4 brown envelopes, barely able to still pass through the narrowing letterbox, and landing always with a thud on the floor. I was sure the post lady was desperate to know the reason that half the load she patiently carried each day came to my house, but she never asked why. As Emily's files were getting thicker and thicker, we both wondered what else could possibly be dragged up in one last attempt to get me locked away in an institution, where the help I was told I needed, would come.

All we required was positive reports from both Cafcass and Dr Somerville to secure the final residence order for all four children. The interim residence order was already in my hands, and Harry, Annie, Alfred and Alice could surely not be removed from my care without these findings failing me miserably? It would have been lovely to have known that I could follow what 'fair play' spoke to my mind, but history was at the fore of my consciousness. I knew I could not trust that justice would come, just because logic said it should.

After a long drawn out year starting with the children's initial removal, a few weeks intimated 'minimal' time to wait. In a similar way to pregnancy though, time seemed to slow down and the nearer I got to the end, the days extended painfully into an eternity in pace. I was sure the clock at this stage added intervals between each hour. The minutes were ticking so slowly, they dragged like a wind-up toy that struggled to keep going on its last leg of every turn.

The children were with me and brought great enjoyment to my day, but the thought never left my mind for one instant, that they could disappear one last time. Each moment I saw their faces, I was reminded that the system I faced, combined with the fighting determination my husband displayed, could result in them leaving. By now they had been home for thirteen weeks and settled as they had before, into all they loved both in the vicinity of the neighbour-hood and the home they adored. However the consternation of all they had been through was expressively present and I was aware it would take years for deep inner healing to manifest a change in the fear that invaded every fibre of their being. Annie would grab me, trembling whenever we left the house in dread that someone would snatch her and take her away. Alfred still clung to me and would never leave my side and Harry displayed the strength of an ox, reflecting his sheer determination to make it through each day. What troubled me was that if they were taken again, I didn't think they would ever heal and be the people they were born to be.

My mind switched to both foster and adoptive homes and I realised for the first time that no matter where a child is placed, to be ripped away from parents whom they love, is one of the great-est travesties of our modern day time. No other home, no amount of external love, no 'better environment', no amount of wisdom, knowledge or experience can replace the bond between a child and its natural loving parent. I hoped to dear God that no report would influence a decision to again take mine.

Following the children's latest return via the court at the beginning of July, Harry, Annie and Alfred had been ordered, as part of the ruling, to holiday with their father and grandparents for a two week period. I felt it was a wrong decision made by the judge, as the children needed to settle. No sooner had they had unpacked their bags I was having to explain to three distressed children that they were once more going away. With great discomfort in my heart they were strapped into their father's car, objecting in the same tormented manner as they had in the past long twelve months. Whatever the outcome of the case and whomever the children finally lived with, I believed regular visits with their father were of extreme importance. Nevertheless, the timing meant it was perceived as a third taking and dug deep into the suffering sitting vulnerably close to the surface.

It was unfair and cruel and they did not want to go. They pleaded with me, as they had so many times before and I wished the judge right then could see first-hand the consequence on these little lives, of the ruling she had made. Judges, solicitors, barristers, expert witnesses, Social Services, psychiatrists, Cafcass officers and police all involve themselves in family lives and act, often with presumptuous authority, undermining choices parents would make, or have made, in the best interests of their children. Nowhere however, in my situation, were they ever exposed to the consequence of their judgments. Neither are they at any time ever held accountable; as are we as parents, when we miscalculate or make wrong decisions.

I made an analogy in my mind to the years I had worked with teenagers in schools, where we taught the importance of being answerable for one's actions. We cultivated an environment where students were expected to accept responsibility, for the effects they had on others. As a core foundation of their lives, they were taught to follow through their decisions, whilst owning obligation and culpability. I thought back to my parents' teaching on repentance, where we said sorry in response to the conviction we had done or said something wrong. I recalled society rules which state so clearly that we consider the effects of our behaviour on those around us and accordingly impose judicial sentences on anyone found guilty of crime.

Here, however, where a breach of basic human rights birthed injustice, deceit, hypocrisy, persecution and cruelty, it became inconsequential. 'Doing something wrong' I realised was of no relevance when no law had been broken. Historically, laws were written by white middle class men to protect themselves. Hence acting in an erroneous or abusive manner was of no consequence in our judicial system, even though the lives of three small children had been wrecked by a representative from almost every profession in the justice arena.

It was an agonising wait but as sure as day became night and night became day, there was a knock on the door and the report arrived by registered mail. I read page after page of Dr Somerville's assessments on both Jonathan and me; the envelope so fat that the post lady this time could not push it through the letterbox, hard though she tried. I had trained myself to skim read well over recent months, as it had become too hard to absorb with such frequency all that was so negatively written about me. I applied this new technique to the pages in front of me, like a bird hovering from a height, looking for a fish in the sea, sifting until something struck my eye.

There were chapters, sections, evidence, analysis, theories, numbers, references, divisions, comparisons and summaries. I flicked my way through my life; behaviour, relationships, ability to mother and set up a home, community, marriage and the whole of this voluminous file. I read sentences that stood out in three dimensions; critical opinions that would be summarised at the end.

The report confirmed that my mother-in-law was responsible

for involving Dr Harwell, without whom, none of the past twelve months could have unfolded. Not only that but it documented she knew him not only professionally, but personally as well. I had been set up by my mother in law and assessed by her friend!

> *"Mrs Dorothy O'Shea, who knows Dr Andrew Harwell professionally and personally, encouraged her son to consult him."*

Dr Somerville, clearly, 'saw through' the underhanded arrangements that had taken place and remarked on the controversial route that my husband had chosen to follow. He mentioned how he had avoided the conventional path of consulting the family GP and the National Health service, a route he suggested, which might have led towards reconciliation. Instead he opted to take himself off to the private system, visiting frequently Dr Harwell's practice in Surrey where he could document his story without having to cope with his wife's contrasting version of events. Dr Somerville implied indignation that Dr Harwell exonerated Jonathan's contribution to the breakdown in our marriage, heaping blame on me when I was not his patient. He wrote that the accusation of an 'alleged' Personality Disorder concerned him.

Scrutinising all the information he had in front of him, he was aware that one side (as in any court case) carried far more truth than the other. He also made it clear that the examination that would take place in court would establish who was more reliable - i.e, whose account was more trustworthy and whose was untrustworthy in greater measure. I browsed over a section touching upon the bias shown toward my husband by the authors of the Cassel Hospital report of May/June 2004. Barely able to inhale for having held my last breath for as long as I could sustain, I perused aloud the fifteen vital words that would be read out in court:

*"She does not suffer from Borderline Personality Disorder
nor any other form of mental illness."*

I continued until I found the words I hoped I needed, for this to
all be okay:

*"I see no reason why this mother is not able to look after
her children."*

My heart raced and tears flowed with jubilation and I hugged the children knowing they would not at this time understand the significance
of my embrace. Warm water rolled down my cheeks reminiscent of
the rivers that had already been shed, as I celebrated so joyfully the
words which I read again and again, to check I wasn't wrong. I hoped
the doubt in my own mind would now possibly vanish.

It had been exactly a year since the first of the many mental
health assessments had been requested by Social Services, which had
been marked as 'urgent'. I joked with friends in the village at the
ridiculousness of how many assessments anyone should need, as we
calculated the number I had now endured. We decided that if we
added Dr Harwell's unethical diagnosis into our recent audit, then
I was averaging a mental health assessment once every two months,
for a whole year's duration. As absurd though it seemed, I at least
carried a certificate, like a warrant of fitness on a car, to prove I was
not mentally ill! We chuckled as I declared I was the only one of
my friends who knew for sure I had a clean bill of health, as far as
my mental state was concerned. Tongue in cheek I suggested each
report framed would make an interesting conversation point if hung
on my sitting room wall! I was pleased I could see the humorous
side of all that had gone on.

The village celebrated my ability to remain 'sane', which counted
as significant, because they were the ones who knew me on a day to

day basis. It became a good discussion point as we all met together and jokes came in thick and fast, as though I were the latest topic of conversation for the day. In truth it was not humorous, but we all needed to let our hair down, and support one another through the intensity of the worry and concern for the children. The odd laugh kept a smile on all of our faces, preventing us tumbling any further than we had already fallen. However, I was not out of the woods yet and we all knew the hurdles I still had to face, but it was lovely to feel some relief and let out some of the stress I had held onto for so long. It was memorable too, to be able to share with such special people in my life, who had committed to being alongside me, during very dark times.

The interval between Doctor Somerville's writings and the arrival of the Cafcass report was not too prolonged. I was grateful for the days I could spend with the children cherishing each moment as though it might be the last. I tried to not let my fear show, as they needed so desperately all the stability that could be provided. I made no mention either, of the fact these could be our last ever days together, playing and enjoying everything that we did.

We spent time doing 'normal' things, as I focused on the repetitive daily events such as fun in the bath and stories at bedtime. We chuckled together, held each other and felt the warmth return as we bonded back into a little unit, readjusting to the loss of their father, but the refreshing arrival of their beloved, beautiful, new baby sister.

It was suddenly only a few days to go until the final court hearing and I cautiously opened the Cafcass report, feeling the same trepidation I had experienced a few days earlier, with a similar size envelope now vehemently sitting on my lap. I had already received a call from Emily to ask if I had heard any news, as she was writing her final affidavit to the court. We needed to meet to go through with a fine tooth comb, the next act in this long drawn out play that would be the finale in the show. She was nervous and asked me how I thought the Cafcass officer would decide. She questioned what position I thought she would take and if I had picked up any hint on which side of the fence she would sit. I admitted I was not decisive, having absolutely no idea what on earth would be written. I reminded her that although I thought I had presented well in the Cassel Hospital assessments, I had presumed incorrectly as it had all turned out disastrously in the end.

The writers at the Cassel had been documented by the court to have been heavily influenced by Doctor Harwell, whose reports they had in their hands. He was a man who had been heavily influential in our case and I had no idea if he was still in communication with Jonathan. I imagined my husband needed all the help he could get, if he was to permanently remove the children from my care. Certainly if he didn't manage to do so, a lot of people were going to have damaged reputations from the wrong allegations they had made. Sadly I didn't have enough faith in the system to believe all could run smoothly so I could not reassure Emily that all was well. Neither did I trust the outcome would rely on the truth. I had not only seen, but also learnt from my experience, that flawed allegations can be made, and unfounded, misguided and invalid wording can result in a court ruling to remove children, without the need for evidence to back it up.

The 'what if' never left my mind. I communicated to Emily that although I knew what the officer 'should' write, I could never be sure that something had not 'popped up' last minute and the other party would be up to new devious tricks. Emily was not any less emotional or passionate than me, and I liked and respected her gutsiness and relentless determination, that thus far had never wavered in my case. She believed in me. She had put herself out with many long hours and sleepless nights, to write endless submissions for court appearances and she would fight to the end.

I honoured Emily as a family lawyer who specialised in child abduction, but more so for her heart for human rights, being passionate in her work with missing and exploited children. She was awarded the inaugural UNICEF Child Rights Lawyer award in 1999. Then in 2002, in recognition for her services to international child abduction and adoption, she was presented with an OBE, in the Queen's New Year's Honours List. Later in 2004 she was selected as Legal Aid Lawyer of the Year for her work with the victims of forced marriage. She was later to receive the 'International Bar Association's Outstanding International Woman Lawyer Award. She worked tirelessly and deserved the recognition for her achievements, as well as her expertise, experience, wisdom, knowledge, integrity, courage and determination.

As Emily had not yet received a copy of the latest Cafcass report in her office, I flipped through the pages with the phone precariously balanced under my ear. I came across comments saying that Jonathan was adamant I remained a potential danger for the children. He suggested the children should live with him immediately and the baby be abruptly weaned. One of his reasons was he felt the children were able to misbehave with him because, "they feel safe to do so." In response the officer noted that she did not observe the rivalries of the same intensity with the mother, as she witnessed with the father. Neither did she sense that the children feared misbehaving in my presence but to the contrary saw no reason whatsoever that I could not meet the children's needs in the foreseeable future.

As I read on, I was thrilled to note she had picked up on Jonathan's misuse of the Cassel report as being of particular concern. She described furthermore how it had been documented that he had shockingly told Harry that the children were to be returned to the mother against his wishes and only so that he could 'avoid arrest'.

I found a section which described a gathering of the 'experts' in accordance with the order of 20 September 2004. The Cafcass officer had convened a meeting between Dr Somerville of the Henderson Hospital and Dr Kimberly of the Cassel Hospital with both of his colleagues who had prepared the family assessments. It stated that although their reports had come to different conclusions; following detailed discussion together, they found themselves largely in agreement. This was partly a result of the Cassel team's dismay, of the father using the report to remove the children from the mother in June. As a consequence, they suggested that the father could benefit from therapeutic help, due to his passive-aggressive, neurotic difficulties. They made it clear that it was:

> *"Inappropriate and irresponsible for the Cassel report to have been used to effect the abrupt removal of the children from their mother."*

In bigger writing, as though in three-dimensions, I then read the words:

> *"The best outcome for the children is for them not to be moved again; removal from the mother is not indicated as at present there is no risk of significant harm to the children."*

Uninterested in the reasons, evidence or findings, I turned to the last few pages to the Cafcass officer's recommendations. I murmured a few odd words to my solicitor, suggesting that I was near to announcing the decision made. There was no hesitancy in the officer's writing. There was no doubt, no concern and as black and white as the colours could be, the recommendation was that the children reside with me. It stated categorically that there was no evidence to support Jonathan's application for the children to be removed from me. Harry, Annie, Alfred and Alice were to remain resident with their mother for the long term!

That was it! Not only had Doctor Somerville produced evidence in my favour, but the long and exhausting investigation that had taken place by court appointed specialists over the last few weeks, climaxed with a recommendation to the court that the children were not to be removed again. Emily was as blown away as me, and I could hear her relief in the sigh that came down the phone; picking up I was sure, the frequency or vibrations that would suggest stress leaving not only her body, but mine as well.

The significance of this report must be the tipping point that would ensure I could not lose my children again. Thrill struck as though an unexpected firework had landed before me exploding in wonderment. Emily conjectured what the response would be from Jonathan, suggesting his legal team should advise him to not continue the fight, but being unsure he would agree.

I wondered if that could possibly be the case, from a law firm that had made more money from him, than the current value of our house. Sure enough though, within a matter of days we heard that he had indeed accepted both proposals that the children permanently reside with me. Our appearance at Kingston County Court therefore was simply to stamp the final residence order with my name on it and seal the conditions of contact.

It was over. It was three hundred and eighty two days from the day when the children were first taken away from their home. Not only were they back with me, but it was in the knowledge that never again could they ever go.

The relief was not for me, or for what I had gained, but for the children who deserved an end to the horrendous time they had been subjected to, for a long year of their lives. Harry, Annie, Alfred and Alice could live in their own home with their mother. They could remain in their schools alongside their friends and we could all continue the reintegration process not only into the geographic location of where we lived, but into the childhood they had been robbed of and the life they deserved.

I could hear the angels again celebrate in heaven with a triumphant praise of joy, and see the stars in the sky shine more radiantly, as my heart enlarged within me and I held my children as I had never done before. It was a hold that retained no fear, as in my hands I held a piece of paper that would secure the future of all of our lives and vindicate me from the lies and accusations that had come my way. Doctor Harwell's so called diagnosis had been disproved, the 'Blue File' had come to nothing, the Cassel report had been torn apart, I was not mentally ill and I had not abused my children. More importantly than all of that put together, Harry, Annie, Alfred and Alice now had a future of hope, anchored in my determination to give them the best lives I could. I was never going to be a perfect mum, but I was determined to do my best. I would love them as naturally and as tenderly as I had always tried to do.

The next chapter could begin and we were free from the control, manipulation, expectation and direction of all those who had been negatively involved in our lives. I felt suddenly proud of my four beautiful children and knew we would make it to have adventures together of the most unbelievable kind. I made a decision there and then, that I would not let this experience affect the lives we were to lead. Whatever healing needed to happen would begin from this day on and would be the catalyst to open doors that had become locked in us all.

The journey would be long, but we were not alone. The rebuilding could commence and I knew the love that was between us would be foundational in breaking through, to be the light that would shine and be the lamp that would guide our path.

CHAPTER TWENTY-FIVE

In November 2003, four weeks after our final court appearance, I contacted Social Services and asked for full core assessments to be carried out on all four children at home. After a two month period they were complete and in my view, all truthfully and honestly written by a newly appointed social worker. They reflected the health and welfare of the children, their environment, family, development, physical, emotional, mental and social wellbeing, schooling and provision. There were four in-depth reports filed and not one found any flaw with my parenting. Neither was any fault found in any statement made by the professionals they interviewed, including the children's teachers, early years' professionals and health workers. In the absence of any criticism, the four reports were extremely complimentary and commented on the high standard of care, balanced with a happy, fun environment in which the children were being raised.

Following the receipt of these reports, I took Social Services to the highest level of complaints and was awarded £500 in compensation. It was offered:

'For any distress caused.'

With it came an unreserved apology for the poor service received by my family and I. No outside, independent body at that time was able to scrutinise the work of Social Services. This meant I was not able to sue them or petition against their actions and they remained accountable to no one.

I took Dr Harwell to the General Medical Council in 2005. The case examiner's decision was that no action would be taken against Dr Harwell's registration as a result of my complaint. Dr Harwell was not given a warning following the outcome of the investigation.

Following the close of the court case, a peace returned to our household and we began to rebuild the broken segments of our lives. A bond developed between the children and I that united us even more closely as a family, and as trust was re-established they began to feel safe once more in our home.

St Margaret's as a community of shop keepers, families and businesses, were extraordinary in pulling together to support the children, in both their schooling, private and social lives. Orleans Infant School and later St Stephen's School, became pivotal in securing a nurturing and enriching environment, in which the children could thrive, with affectionate, supportive teachers. The care they received from all of the staff could never be faulted.

Weekend visits with the children's father remained hard for their young years. 'Hand-overs' continued to trigger anxiety and trauma from association with past events. However, we had to count our blessings and remain positive that one day change to the court system would mean judges would look more favourably about awarding unsupervised staying contact with 'taking parents', without measuring the consequence.

To this day I remain perplexed about Jonathan and his parents' real motivation for wanting sole custody of the children. My experience has highlighted the flaws in the english justice system that allows the controlling, wealthy and knowledgeable to manipulate it to fulfill their own desires. It is time that the system is critically examined to ensure justice is available for all, including innocent children who have limited voice, when the 'left behind' parent has no access to funds.

EPILOGUE

In 2011, following the loss of my dear father and with permission from the court, I moved to New Zealand with Harry, Annie, Alfred and Alice to live near my sister Belle. All four children are thriving as we continue to live under the promise that the past would be the catalyst for generating a better future. Their father has since moved to Singapore and sees the children regularly.

In Auckland we have had the opportunity to live on the edge of the water, with kayaks at the bottom of our garden and a jetty where the children dive on hot summer's days. We have camped each summer on golden sandy beaches in some of the most beautiful, deserted settings in the world. We have also found time to explore the Southern Hemisphere, having wonderful adventures together as all four have grown. The children have all sailed and windsurfed becoming proficient on New Zealand's open seas and have made the most of opportunities that we would never have had in London.

At the time of publishing this book the children are 11, 13, 15 and 17. The trauma played out in their lives as I foresaw in 2003/4, and they have all undergone professional therapy to support their journeys. As a measure of their bravery and courage and as a reflection of their positive young spirits, they have gone on to shine as young adults.

Harry has recently completed his Gold Duke of Edinburgh Award, having committed to three years of service in the community, a sport and a skill. He has also completed many arduous tramps as a measure of his focus, reliability, commitment and ability to endure under tough physical, emotional and psychological conditions. He is a keen windsurfer, plays tennis and squash and is a charming, positive and thoughtful young man, with a humour that delights us all. He is currently in his last year at school and has applied to University to fulfill his dream of becoming an engineer.

Annie sings in the Auckland Girls Choir, as well as two school choirs. She plays the guitar well and is a proficient dancer and sportswoman. She has also participated in the Bronze and Silver Duke of Edinburgh Programme and is about to embark on her Gold Award. She is highly competent in her academic studies; achieving top grades in most subjects. Annie is sensitive and caring and has grown into a beautiful and talented young woman, bringing sophistication, beauty and grace to everything around.

Alfred's fierce determination has been channelled into becoming an awesome drummer, as well as one of the best young windsurfers in the area. He plays hockey for the school and astounds us all with his passionate love of all things in trees! From his tool box he has enterprisingly hand crafted ladders, ropes to swing on, and zip wires that take his friends from one side of the garden to another. A handsome young man, as well as a talented dancer, he has a scientific mind and his conviction will take him far.

Alice surprised us all. The stress of my pregnancy revealed no negative consequences and she has bounced through life with not a care in the world. If ever Social Services were to look at her they would wonder at the conviction of the words they once wrote. About to embark on her secondary schooling, she is a keen netball player, and an excellent swimmer. She loves playing the guitar and is showing great artistic talent and flair. Easy going and energetic in her gentle nature, she brings much joy to those around her.

Following the completion of *Taken*, I have written a second book, which chronicles how we made strides in overcoming adversity to live rich abundant lives. It will be published in the near future. I spent some time teaching Restorative Justice in UK prisons, observing first hand, some of the travesties of our justice system, which has opened my eyes to the suffering inflicted on the vulnerable and marginalised in our society. I am currently involved in prophetic ministry and work as a life coach, being passionate about seeing trauma and suffering as a catalyst to bring change and transformation in broken lives.

The anguish we went through in 2003/4 has taught us many valuable life lessons; namely the actions and words of others do not dictate who we are and what we are to become. We are all created as perfect, divine individuals with a purpose and plan for our lives. It is only in breaking free from the connection to an individual's opinion of us, that we can step in and find our true identity in who we really are. The insecurity of others; their mind-sets, behaviour patterns and words they choose to use do not confine us, limit us or restrict us, nor do the actions they take. Moreover, if we find our true uniqueness; and walk in the authority of who we are, then nothing can deter us from having totally fulfilled lives. An understanding of 'suffering' is foundational in reminding us, that our strength does not come from what we surround ourselves with, nor in what we achieve. When we are stripped bare of all attachment to both people and things, and even robbed of our basic human rights, we can then begin to see with fresh eyes what truly matters in life. For the children and I, that is the gift of each day, the provision and abundance we live in, and the blessing of knowing love in its purest form. As a family we are grateful for having been propelled further into our destiny. We live in the truth that the gift of life is a blessing for us all.

About the Author

Sue O'Callaghan lives in Auckland, New Zealand, with her four children; Harry, Annie, Alfred and Alice.

Born the middle of three girls, in Bedfordshire, England, she has travelled the world and experienced life in many capacities. An accomplished artist and experienced teacher, she inspires many through her desire to see the lives of others transformed.

Her inspiring story, involving having her children removed from her through false accusations, is the basis on which she claims that all difficult life circumstances can be seen as a trigger to catapult one into a life of rich blessing and abundance. Her tenacity to fight for her children's return, combined with her passion for life, are a truly motivating fusion which draw others to her love of all things.

Sue's artistic eye and affection for beauty is seen not only in the physical environment she creates, but also in her vision for the lives of others.

"Without love", she says, "there can be no compassion. It is compassion that brings life to all things."